Ask The Animals

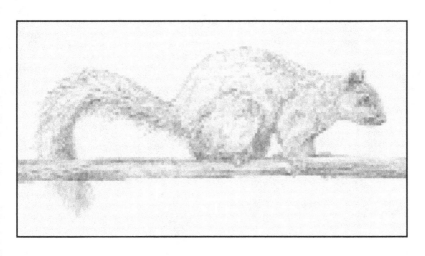

Also by the author:

Pilgrimage to Priesthood

Praying the Bible

Journaling with Jeremiah

Heart Whispers

A Table of Delight

Ask The Animals

Spiritual Wisdom From All God's Creatures

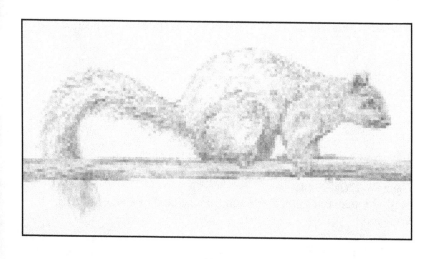

Elizabeth J. Canham

MOREHOUSE PUBLISHING

HARRISBURG · NEW YORK

Unless otherwise noted, the Scripture quotations contained herein are from the New Revised Standard Version Bible, copyright © 1989 by the Division of Christian Education of the National Council of Churches of Christ in the U.S.A. Used by permission. All rights reserved.

Morehouse Publishing, P.O. Box 1321, Harrisburg, PA 17105

Morehouse Publishing, 445 Fifth Avenue, New York, NY 10016

Morehouse Publishing is an imprint of Church Publishing Incorporated.

Cover art by Dorothy Thompson Perez

Cover design by Wesley Hoke

Interior design by Irene Zevgolis

Library of Congress Cataloging-in-Publication Data

Canham, Elizabeth, 1939-
  Ask the animals : spiritual wisdom from all God's creatures / Elizabeth J. Canham.
    p. cm.
  ISBN-13: 978-0-8192-2232-9 (pbk.)
  1. Animals—Religious aspects—Christianity. I. Title.
  BT746.C36 2006
  242—dc22
                                    2006025426
Printed in the United States of America

06 07 08 09   10 9 8 7 6 5 4 3 2 1

Dedication

This book is dedicated to Bonnie
1986 – 12.13.03

Wise Teacher
Spiritual Guide
Companion
Hunter
Lover
Friend

Contents

Acknowledgments

I am grateful for all the four-legged, winged, and finned creatures who have blessed my life and taught me wisdom. Many of them appear in this book but I would add Brigid, Sally, Gyp, Tibby, Tigger, Meg, Teebone, Colin, Sammy, Holly, Jack, Bell, Brighty, and Lemur. Gratitude is also due to my English teacher in Secondary School, Miss Jessie Crowther, who believed in my ability to write despite the ink-stained, misspelled work I turned in to her. I offer thanks for poets and environmentalists whose work has touched me deeply, especially Mary Oliver, Thomas Berry, Hafiz, R. S. Thomas, Rumi, and Kathleen Norris.

I am also grateful to Nancy Fitzgerald, my editor, who has offered wise guidance and encouragement during the writing of this book.

Preface

"Let everything that breathes praise the Lord!"—Psalm 150:6

The Hebrew Scriptures offer many poetic images of creation and the Creator's purpose and joy in all that comes to be. As each new phase of creation unfolds, God proclaims, "It is good." And when humanity arrives on the scene, the Creator entrusts the care of all that has been made into our hands. The narrator ends this account of creation by adding, "God saw everything that [God] had made, and indeed, it was very good" (Genesis 1:31).

All throughout the Bible, the focus on all living things continues. Jesus frequently uses images of creatures and creation in his teaching. But the story of human progress and struggle, faithlessness and beginning again becomes the prime emphasis in the sacred text, and often we forget our dependence on—and responsibility for—creation. Today, as natural resources dwindle and hunger is a daily reality for so many, we are compelled to own our greed and failure to accept the responsibility that is ours, so that God may, once again, look at creation and proclaim, "It is good."

But there is more than this. The creation and creatures we have neglected are gifted with the wisdom we need. Animals, especially, invite our attention and honor because their essential nature is mostly devoid of the kind of pretense we have learned to practice in cultural and religious life. If they are angry, they express anger; when joy fills them, they live their joy; and when danger approaches, they recognize it for what it is and take action. Animals express deep care for their young, know how to find and enjoy food, accept their limitations, and live in harmony with the rhythms of day and night, times and seasons. Jesus specifically tells his listeners to observe the birds: "Do not worry about your life, what you will eat or what you will drink, or about your body, what you will wear. Is not life more than food, and the body more than clothing? Look at the birds of the air; they neither sow nor reap nor gather into barns, and yet your heavenly Father feeds them. Are you not of more value than they?" (Matthew 6:25–26). If we took the message of Jesus seriously, the food and fashion industries might have to rethink their strategies for persuading us to crave their products.

These reflections are the fruit of two loves, two teachers: Scripture and animals. My love for the Hebrew and Christian Scriptures was nurtured in a very conservative tradition that took the Bible literally and taught that humans were to subdue creation. My love for animals was a gift from my mother, who tenderly lifted earthworms from harm's way, though she feared their wriggling bodies.

This love that my mother taught me was kept underground for many years as I defended an infallible Bible and the Sovereign God who authored it. My spiritual journey has led me away from this early, rigid approach to Scripture, but my joy in the sacred text increased as I learned to allow the various writers to inhabit their own time and culture. I celebrate the porous nature of the biblical narratives that allow me to find truth that is both enduring and relevant to the present moment because they are not locked in the past. With this fresh understanding of Scripture, I also learned to read from God's "other book"—creation. I now understand how St. Anthony could point to the rugged mountains surrounding his cave -dwelling and answer a philosopher who asked how he would pray without a copy of the Scriptures, "Creation will be my book." Mother was right.

In the last few years, animals have increasingly arrested my attention and taught me more about the Creator. After an encounter with humpback whales that reduced me to tears of awe and mystery, I remarked to my bishop that the experience "was much more wor-shipful than church usually is." He did not fire me; he also knew the God-presence manifested powerfully in creation as he hiked in the mountains that are dear to both of us. When I have preached or offered retreats, I have felt compelled to share stories of animal encounters to illuminate Scripture. The response has been positive; often, listeners have expressed gratitude that the role and blessing of God's creatures is being honored in Christian tradition. Many I speak with have a tenuous relationship with organized religion, often because they have felt abused by a church that used the Bible moralistically and denied the value of personal experience and questions. They have turned to God's other book, preferring time in the midst of creation to pew-bound Sunday mornings. Others who have remained in the church ask why we have often been so self-focused that we have failed to recall and receive the wisdom of the whole created order. I hope that the vignettes of animal encounters I recount in this book will appeal to both groups and that each of us, through animal encounters, may deepen our relationship with the Source of all Being.

No less a biblical luminary than Job understood this. When Job's trite and insensitive "friends" suggest that his wickedness has led to the many disasters that befall him, he refuses their simplistic theology and makes it clear that nothing happens unless God allows it. There are bad people who do not suffer punishment, robbers who live at peace while god-fearing people are made a laughingstock. "Ask the animals," Job says, "and they will teach you; the birds of the air, and they will tell you . . . who among all these does not know that the hand of the Lord has done this?" (Job 12:7, 9). God's wisdom is greater than ours, and Job refuses to believe that God is punishing him for evil. Even the animals, he insists, acknowledge the inscrutable purposes of the Creator—so ask *them* what is going on.

The meditations that follow emerged as I allowed animals to teach me. Some readers may wish to use these thirty reflections as daily readings for a month. Others may prefer to note the theme associated with each animal story and select one that is appropriate to their prayer focus. By offering my own experience of praying with animals, I invite readers to explore the wonderful wisdom of animals for themselves and to enter into an ever-deepening relationship with the Creator through joyful presence with "all creatures great and small."

Mystery

God's Playmates

The Hebrew Scriptures begin with a great panorama that catches our imagination and takes our breath away. We come into being in deep, dark chaos over which the Spirit of God broods, waiting to give birth. The first dawn breaks as the Creator sends a wind over the void and Light comes to give definition to day and night. And God sees that it is good. Then the gift of water flows, its power harnessed as plants, trees, and living creatures of earth, air, and ocean dance into view. Again, God observes that it is good. The finale celebrates the decision of God to create beings that reflect the divine image, and it is to them that the Creator entrusts care for all that has come to be. We look with God at everything that has been made, and indeed, it is very good (Genesis 1:31).

The story of creation plunges us into Mystery. The narrative invites our wonder and our worship, our joy and celebration of the interconnected web that is the universe—beyond our understanding but not beyond our imagination. When I read this narrative, I imagine myself in a darkened theater, waiting breathlessly for the curtain to rise, overwhelmed by the beauty, majesty, and amazing creativity of God as scene after scene is played out. The final chorus brings us to our feet as a standing ovation goes on and on—it is all good, indeed, very good. We close our Bibles, leave the drama, and go

outside with regret that the end has come—only to discover that Creation is all around us to remind us constantly of God's very good work. Rain falls, then the sun comes out; birds sing and trees blossom; otters play in the river and the dog leaps with barks of ecstasy to celebrate our homecoming. Indeed, it is very good.

Mystery is all around us and at the heart of our own being, but we become so accustomed to what is around us that we fail to see and be filled with awe—anywhere, not just in places of scenic wonder. For several years I lived in a tiny apartment in New York City where the early-morning sounds were garbage trucks rumbling down the street, a far cry from the birdsong I had learned to love. At first, I resented the absence of natural beauty, but soon learned to notice the amazing resilience of the earth and the presence of creatures, including the ubiquitous cockroaches. I felt my heart lighten one morning as I stood at a gridlocked intersection where the sound of curses and car horns filled the air and, looking up, noticed a row of pigeons perched on the long arm of a traffic signal from which they observed the human chaos. Were they laughing at us? They certainly invited my gratitude and taught me to "lighten up" and rise above the dust and debris that polluted my sense of wonder. The sidewalk where I waited to catch the downtown bus was buckled where weeds had pushed through the concrete, offering a powerful image of creation's victory in oppressive circumstances. Even inside my apartment, I had plants and flowers and a collection of natural objects to help me pray through the distractions of city life.

That morning was one of those occasions when we experience Mystery so powerfully that the grace of the moment is truly amazing. I've been blessed to experience many other such moments. Soon after I moved to the United States from England in 1981, I visited a friend on Cape Cod. From Boston, I boarded a ferry to Provincetown; about midway across the bay, the captain announced that a whale had been sighted, so he stopped the boat and passengers crowded at the rails to watch. Sure enough, a telltale water spout rose into the air followed by the great, dark shape of a humpback whale. We watched for several minutes, oblivious to friends awaiting our late arrival on the Cape. Then and there I fell in love with these great creatures of the deep. During the week I spent with my friend, we went on a whale-watch vessel that took us out of Provincetown harbor to the deep waters off Stellwagen Bank, where the whales were known to feed. We saw many whales that day, including one of the few endangered right whales, and the marine biologist on board explained the importance of monitoring the habits and migratory patterns of whales. Humpback whales were being identified by the underside of their tails, which all had different and unique markings that led to their naming by the Center for Marine Biology.

One big humpback whale was feeding alongside her calf, and as we came close, I was awed by her gentleness and beauty. I learned that some of the support for research came from ordinary people like me who "adopted" a whale of their choice, so I immediately signed up to adopt this wonderful mother, whose name was Salt. Over the years I received reports of sightings of Salt and her offspring as they returned each year from the Caribbean—it was an exciting day when I learned that she had become a grandmother.

I am drawn back again and again to be among whales in their natural habitat, and my awe has increased as I have learned more about them. Though their longevity and breeding patterns remain a mystery to scientists, I think I understand the wonderful sense of playfulness that led God to make Leviathan—the great whale of Scripture—to sport in the ocean (Psalm 104:26). The writers of the Talmud, the ancient writings of the rabbis on Jewish law and tradition seem to agree: "For three hours of each day, God amuses Himself (sic) so to speak, with the Leviathan"[1] (Avodah Zarah 3b). Whales are God's playmates. I long to join God with the whales— diving, breaching, caring for their young, entirely at home in the deep ocean, but the closest I come to that dream is standing at the side of a boat. These days, I leave my camera behind—attempts to frame the moment rob me of the exhilaration that comes from being truly present to the vision of the divine these lovely animals embody.

Some days I'm blessed with more of these moments than others. On a day in 2001 my shipmates and I were rewarded with the sighting of a young whale breaching repeatedly. As we began to head back to harbor, the biologist on board observed two more whales he'd seen traveling together at the beginning of the season, both of them apparently pregnant and staying together for protection. Their journey together reminded me of Mary's journey to her cousin Elizabeth whose baby, John the Baptist, leaped in her womb in joyful recognition of the mother of Jesus. One of the pregnant whales, it turned out, was Salt. Though I missed her first sighting that day, she and her companion quickly reappeared. Slowly Salt separated herself from her companion and came toward the boat until she was lying, full length, alongside, just a few feet below where I stood. As I write these words, tears of awe and joy prickle once more behind my eyelids. Salt and I were united once again, and I sensed a connection that is far deeper than words can express or the human mind can understand. It was a holy moment, an

---

1. Rabbis Nosson Scherman and Meir Zlotowitz, eds. *Tehillim* (vol. 2; New York: Mesorah Publications, 1977), 1264i.

encounter with the Mystery at the heart of the universe, and a moment when I felt as Moses must have felt when he knew the presence of God as he stood beside the burning bush. In this divine encounter, I stepped out of the shoes of rationality to stand, tears of joy running down my windblown face, in the awesome, mysterious presence of God. Indeed, it was very good.

REFLECTING WITH SCRIPTURE
Genesis 28:10–17
Can you recall moments in your life when the awesome Mystery of God has been revealed to you? How did you respond? Are there ways you might become more conscious of holy Presence in daily life?

PRAYER
Mysterious Creator of all things living, we offer thanks for the amazing world you made and for blessing us as caretakers. May we never lose a sense of wonder as we walk the holy ground of this earth. When we forget you, please surprise us with your near presence in creatures who invite our playfulness and worship. Amen.

Faith

What's the Buzz?

One afternoon, shortly after I moved to the United States, I sat on the tiled porch of an elegant South Carolina plantation house. The spring air was warm, and a light breeze wafted fragrance from a bed of multicolored blooms as I rocked drowsily beside one of the great white pillars. This must be what heaven is like, I thought—no more of that chilly British rain or fog-filled days and gray skies for me. I was startled out of my reverie by a very loud buzzing sound, and saw, just above the flowers, the biggest bug I had ever laid eyes on. Incredulously I watched as it seemed suspended above one of the larger blooms and dipped its head deep into the center of the flower. Then it rose, hovered, and moved on to begin the nectar-gathering process all over again. I had just met my first hummingbird.

The ruby-throated hummingbird is a regular visitor to my home in the North Carolina mountains. Since my shady yard does not boast many fragrant, nectar-filled plants, I suspend feeders filled with sugar water close to the window where I can watch these extraordinary, tiny birds. Their rapid, humming wing beat enables them to hover as they feed and also to fly backward if necessary. They can be aggressive little birds, chasing rivals away from the feeder and somehow avoiding the midair collisions that are a traffic controller's nightmare. One day, I walked onto my screen porch

where I heard a whirring, buzzing sound and discovered that one of the humming birds, no doubt attempting to escape a competitor, had failed to notice that it was heading at high speed toward the screen. The bird's long beak had penetrated the mesh and stuck. The hummingbird's helicopter wings beat frantically, but it was unable to extricate itself from the tight fibers. It took less than a second for me to apply light pressure on the protruding beak and push the humming bird backward into freedom.

In early spring one year, I looked out the window and there, hovering in space, was a disappointed humming bird reproachfully waiting for food. Clearly it had returned to the precise place where it had previously found a plentiful supply of nectar. The bird had enough faith to migrate back to my yard and was making irritated, squeaky "chipping" sounds to alert me to its hunger. I quickly made up some nectar and filled the feeder. "Faith is the assurance of things hoped for," the little bird's life proclaimed; "the conviction of things not seen" (Hebrews 11:1). That bird appeared to be endowed with a faith that, despite not seeing nectar at the moment of return, knew that it would find its needs met again. I was reminded of those many occasions when I return to my daily practice of reading Scripture expecting to be "fed," only to discover that distractions, and perhaps tiredness, leave me feeling empty and unsatisfied. Faith means that I will not give up. I will keep "hovering" over the Word of God until it yields the soul food for which I long. Faith means that I continue to trust in God, perhaps squeaking a bit to make sure I am heard, until I am satisfied.

One of the more difficult passages in the Gospel according to Matthew appears to portray Jesus as insensitive, even racist. A woman from Canaan approaches him because her daughter is sick and she had heard of Jesus' healing ministry. "Have mercy on me, Lord, Son of David; my daughter is tormented by a demon" (Matthew 15:22). Jesus ignores the woman, and finally the disciples plead with him to send her away since she is now making them uncomfortable with her persistent shouting for attention. Jesus says that his mission is to the "lost sheep of the house of Israel," but the woman does not give up. In a response that seems even ruder than the first, Jesus says, "It is not fair to take the children's food and throw it to the dogs." She replies, "Yes, Lord, yet even the dogs eat the crumbs that fall from the masters' table." Then Jesus answers her, "'Woman, great is your faith! Let it be done for you as you wish.' And her daughter was healed instantly" (13:25–28).

Although the story makes us uncomfortable because it portrays Jesus in a way that seems insensitive to us, the intent is clear: We are to be persistent in prayer and faith. We do not come to Jesus as those who have pride in our origins, but with humility and a willingness to own our poverty. In the time of Jesus, the audacity of this woman would have been shocking; no faithful Jew would speak with a woman in public, even his own wife—but this woman refuses to give up, even when Jesus tries to ignore her. She hovers and squeaks until she gets what she needs and in the process hears Jesus comment on her great faith.

It is hard to be faithful in prayer when God seems to be deaf to our cries for help. Sometimes the psalmists express deep anger at God, who appears to have abandoned them: "How long, O Lord? Will you forget me forever? How long will you hide your face from me?" (Psalm 13:1). For us, too, it may be necessary to pour out our anguish and sense of loss, to allow God to hear our cry of disappointment, in order to pray authentically. In those cries, spoken rather than internalized, there is healing and restoration to faith. "I trusted in your steadfast love; my heart shall rejoice in your salvation. I will sing to the Lord, for he has dealt bountifully with me" (13:5–6). We deepen our faith every time we look at our emptiness and trust that God has not forgotten the nectar.

REFLECTING WITH SCRIPTURE
Hebrews 12:1–2
How do you deal with those times when God seems absent? What steps might you take to strengthen your faith?

PRAYER
Faithful God, remind me to trust in times of loss and to know that my faith is strengthened as I pray with honesty and persistence. Help me to wait for your time and feed me with the sweetness of your grace. Amen.

Hope

Don't Fence Me In

Earnest is a tortoise with an attitude. He lives in England with an animal-loving family who, over the years, have acquired three sheep, two goats, guinea pigs, rabbits, chickens, and numerous dogs and cats. Earnest joined the menagerie in 2003 when he was about thirty-five years-old, and he lives in a section of the yard where the hens wander free. At one end of his pen, he has a cozy, straw-filled shelter, but his exercise area is sometimes intruded on by the hens. When Earnest observes two skinny legs of a chicken nearby, he gathers all his energy and runs—yes, runs; tortoises are not *always* slow—and snaps at the offending intruder. Humans receive a similar treatment, but since his jaws are not wide enough to bite a person, he simply runs, then tucks his head inside his shell and repeatedly bashes their legs. Earnest was born a wanderer and is an ingenious escapee. Every few weeks panic sets in when Earnest has once again gone missing, and a major search ensues throughout the property and beyond. Once, Earnest was given up as totally lost when he was absent for some weeks and a notice was posted on the gate asking passersby to watch out for him. He was discovered, several blocks away, by a vigilant woman who happened to be visiting her mother in the neighborhood and spotted him. He was duly returned to his quarters once more.

Earnest sometimes gets confused about the hibernation habits of his kin. In the fall he will retire to his sleeping area and not be seen for days, but as soon as he is taken into his winter home inside the house, he wakes up and is put back outside. The family gets some respite from the endless attention Earnest requires when he finally does drop off for his long winter sleep, but when spring arrives, various members of the family begin to check on Earnest. When will he wake up? Is he okay? Maybe he died in his sleep. Hope is kept alive by the recollection of all the previous years when Earnest has ended his hibernation and poked his head out of his shell once more to look the world in the face. Hope is rewarded, and the attention cycle begins once again as Earnest tries to dig himself out of his pen, despite ample supplies of carrots and lettuce delivered to his suite each day, as well as regular polishing with olive oil to prevent his shell from drying out in the warm weather.

Neither of Earnest's protectors were enthusiastic about educa-

tion. When Mr. Earnest-Protector left school two years before grad-
uation, the principal added a succinct note at the end of his school
report: I hope! I am not sure what he hoped for. Maybe he hoped
that at a later time Earnest's Protector would return to his education
or, at the very least, acquire a skill that would enable him to support
a family. His hopes have been more than fulfilled. Mr. Earnest
Protector is multiskilled in practical ways; he is a fine cook, and after
many years of working successfully in the retail market, he returned
to school and is now a qualified therapist with special gifts for working with teenagers. Hope became reality, as it does each spring when
Earnest wakes up. Earnest is a demanding guest, but deeply loved
for all that—though the hens may have a different perspective.

The foundation for hope is revealed in the biblical narratives as
God's utter faithfulness and, amazingly, as the trust God places in
us. In a time of turmoil and distress the psalmist addresses God,
saying, "My hope is in you" (Psalm 39:7), and we find stories of hope
scattered throughout Scripture. Abraham and Sarah were old when
they were promised offspring, but after receiving God's promise,
Paul writes in his letter to the Romans: "Hoping against hope, he
believed that he would become the 'father of many nations'"
(Romans 4:18). Paul continues to explore the theme of hope in the
following chapter when he writes: "Suffering produces endurance,
and endurance produces character, and character produces hope, and
hope does not disappoint us, because God's love has been poured
into our hearts through the Holy Spirit that has been given to us"
(Romans 5:3–5). Paul suggests a progression in human response to
difficulty. Suffering is an inevitable reality for all of us, but our
endurance (steadfastness) in the face of pain shapes our character,
which, in turn, produces hope. There is a movement from despair
and faithlessness to the embrace, once again, of God's faithfulness
through all the vicissitudes of our lives.

When we reflect on the stories of those chosen by God to be
prophets and messengers of hope, we find that these men and
women are ordinary people, vulnerable and subject to mistakes.
Abraham lies about Sarah, passing her off as his sister; Jacob flees
home when his deceptions land him in trouble with his family;
Jonah tries to run away when God asks him to go to a people he

despises; Peter, named by Jesus as "the Rock," is anything but rock-like in his discipleship, especially when he denies any connection with Christ. Yet each of these people was used by God for great purposes, and each of them learned, through the pain that shaped their character, to embody hope in the living God.

Let's consider Peter. After the resurrection of Jesus, some of the disciples had joined Peter on a fishing trip. A long, unsuccessful night left them disappointed, tired, and hungry, and they were probably irritated by the stranger standing on the shore shouting his advice about where to fish. We can only imagine their stunned response when their nets filled up. John, perhaps recalling an earlier incident when Jesus was with them and they had miraculously caught fish, realizes that the stranger could be only one person. When he tells the others, Peter immediately jumps out of the boat in his urgent desire to get to Jesus. Despite all his failure, Peter retains some hope that Jesus would still receive him.

On the beach, a charcoal fire burned and fish were cooking on it. The pungent odor of the burning charcoal, reminiscent of the evening when Peter stood before a brazier warming his hands and vehemently denying that he knew Jesus, would surely stir in Peter's memory. Although Jesus had already prepared breakfast, he invites the disciples to bring some of the fish they had caught, validating their gifts. After the meal, Jesus has a question to put to Peter: "Simon son of John, do you love me?" (John 21:15). How was Peter to answer this question, knowing that he had so recently let Jesus down? Jesus had used the word *agapao* from which we derive agape, or love feast, when he spoke to Peter. The disciple replies in the affirmative but uses *phileo* instead—another word for love that's perhaps less intense and more like a brotherly affection. Jesus replies, "Feed my sheep (*arnia*)." The same question and response are repeated, and again Jesus replies, "Feed my sheep," this time changing the word for sheep to *probate*, or little sheep. When the question is asked a third time, the narrative adds, "Peter felt hurt because he said to him the third time, 'Do you love me?'" (John 21:17), and it is often assumed that it is the repetition of the question that upsets Peter. But there is another possibility. When Jesus asks the question the third time, he uses *phileo*, the word for love with which Peter had responded earlier. Perhaps Peter was hurt because Jesus placed a question mark even against the level of love that Peter did claim. Peter says to Jesus: "Lord, you know everything; you know that I love you" (John 21:17).

This story, which ends the Gospel according to John, offers a clear message that, with God, failure is never final. Jesus continues to place his hope in Peter and to see in him a passionate man with the potential for great leadership. Despite Peter's failures, and his frequent misunderstanding of the teaching of Jesus, he was trusted with leadership of the emerging community of faith. On Peter's report card, Jesus inscribed the words "I hope!" The day of Pentecost saw Peter begin his teaching and leadership in the church through the energizing power of the Holy Spirit. Peter was not faultless from that time on, but he knew the power of forgiveness and the hope of beginning again. He knew too that Christ hoped in him because he had woken up to a new springtime and the opportunity to start fresh.

REFLECTING WITH SCRIPTURE
Hebrews 6:9–12
What does God hope for in you?

PRAYER
God of hope and new beginnings, give us grace to remain steadfast in our faith and never lose hope in your mercy. Increase our love for you and help us to live into the dream you have for us and for the world. Make us messengers of hope to all your people. Amen.

Love

If You Want to Keep Your Head — Wear a Hat

The island of Farne lies off the northeast coast of England. It is a wild place, pounded by high seas and notorious for shipwrecks. It is also home to many species of birds who thrive on its rocky ledges and announce their presence by cacophonous cries and the pungent odor of their droppings. Seals breed and sing their mournful songs among eider ducks, gulls, cormorants, puffins, and many other species that make their home in the inhospitable Atlantic islands.

In the seventh-century CE, St. Cuthbert, abbot of the Celtic monastic community on Lindisfarne (Holy Island), fled to Farne in search of solitude. He spent the rest of his life as a hermit, at home in the wildness and isolation of the island and with the creatures who shared his rugged dwelling place. Cuthbert's deep love for, and connection with, animals is attested by stories passed down through the centuries. The best known of these tales relates to the time before Cuthbert left the monastery. One night a brother followed Cuthbert on his nightly walk out into the sea, where he stood for many hours with outstretched arms—the traditional posture for prayer among the Celtic peoples. Retreating from the ocean, Cuthbert was greeted by sea otters who gently rubbed him dry with their fur.

Farne is now a bird sanctuary, and on days when the sea is

relatively calm, a limited number of visitors are permitted to visit the island. Disembarking from the ferry, guests are told that they may only walk along designated paths and must keep the volume of conversation low in order to honor the breeding birds and their habitat. A group of us made the rough crossing one summer and were warned ahead of time to wear hats—not primarily for protection from the ultraviolet rays that penetrate even the gray, windblown clouds, but from the arctic terns whose protective instincts lead to hostile behavior. Fearing that their offspring might be endangered by intruders, the terns divebomb the heads of unsuspecting visitors, sometimes inflicting serious injuries with their sharp beaks. Sure

enough, as soon as we reached the area where the terns nested at
ground level among the foliage, the adult birds flew up, fussing
around us and beginning their repeated assaults on our heads.
Waving arms did not deter them, and when we stooped to look
more closely at the fledglings, the parents increased their diving
raids on our heads. The terns demonstrated fierce love, the kind of
love that will face any danger in order to protect the loved one.

The word "love" has been debased in our culture and is used in
a variety of ways that diminish its meaning. Romantic love is
portrayed night after night on television and is used to sell all kinds
of products; we also speak of loving chocolate, the beach, hats, dogs,
or clothes. As parents and children, we say, "I love you," and the
greeting card industry provides us with endless opportunities to buy
and send the often-sentimental cards they produce. "God is love," we
tell children in Sunday School—and perhaps we have the same
message cross-stitched and hanging on our wall. God *is* love, but we
need to consider what we mean by the phrase. What kind of love is
God? A beautiful passage in Isaiah 43 speaks of the tenderness of
God who loves those created in the divine image: "You are precious
in my sight, and honored, and I love you" (43:4). The prophet Hosea,
who went on loving the wife who was unfaithful to him, suggests
that his experience is a metaphor for God's love for us: God forgives
our abandonment of the covenant of grace, and yearns to receive us
back and embrace us in arms of love. "Therefore, I will now allure
her, and bring her into the wilderness, and speak tenderly to her.
From there I will give her vineyards and make the Valley of Achor a
door of hope. There she shall respond as in the days of her youth, as
at the time when she came out of the land of Egypt" (Hosea
2:14–15). God's love is tender, compassionate, forgiving, and
gracious.

God's love is also fierce and protective, and like "the bear robbed
of her cubs" (Hosea 13:8)—or like the tern risking her own life for
her fledglings—God will repel enemies. God does not love us with
greeting-card sentimentality, but with fierce and passionate caring.
Another image used in Scripture pictures God as the mother eagle
who knows that she must teach her young to fly if they are to
survive. She will not feed them forever. The eagle pushes the young

birds out of the eerie so that they will learn to spread their wings, ride the air currents, and search for food—but she then drops below them and catches them on her wings until they are able to fly on their own. This is tough love, the kind of love God gave to the people of Israel as they struggled through the wilderness after they left Egypt: "I bore you on eagles' wings and brought you to myself" (Exodus 19:4). Ornithologists tell us that if the eaglets refuse to fly after numerous times of being born up on the mother's wings, she will destroy the nest so that they must fly or die. God is tender and gentle like the most caring mother, but will not allow us to remain immature and over dependent. We must be willing to risk and to face our fears knowing that because God loves us, we will never be abandoned.

Jesus tells us that the kind of love God has for us should characterize our relationships within the Christian community also. Jesus spells this out for the disciples when he gathers them together to prepare them to continue his ministry after his departure. In chapters 13 through 17 of John's Gospel, Jesus, in rabbinic style, gives his followers his last will and testament, a discourse rooted in practical love. Jesus begins by washing the disciples' feet, an act of utmost humility, telling them that they are to serve one another in the same way. "As the Father has loved me," Jesus goes on to say, "so I have loved you; abide in my love. If you keep my commandments, you will abide in my love. . . . This is my commandment, that you love one another as I have loved you" (John 15:9–10, 12). The love Jesus displayed reached beyond personal preferences, forgave mistakes, welcomed the unlovable, and led to transformed lives. He showed his love in a special way to those who were unprotected—the poor, women, children, outcasts—and he was uncompromising in his treatment of the perpetrators of abusive behavior, even if they were revered religious leaders—Jesus "pecked" repeatedly at their self-inflated egos and exposed their hypocrisy. God is love, loving us with the fierceness of the tern, the bear, the eagle, and enfolding us in gentleness, forgiveness, and the grace to begin again each time we stumble.

REFLECTING WITH SCRIPTURE
1 Corinthians 13
When have you been aware of God's love for you? How is God's love for others revealed in the world today?

PRAYER
Holy One, we claim as our own your promise to Jeremiah: "I have loved you with an everlasting love, therefore I have continued my faithfulness to you" (31:3). We give thanks for the tough love through which you have enabled us to grow, and for the tender, enfolding love in which you hold us when we are lost or afraid. Help us to love one another as you have loved us and to show that love by our patience, kindness, and humility toward our sisters and brothers. May the world, through us, be given a vision of your commonwealth of justice, peace, and love. Amen.

Humility

Little Things Mean a Lot

I think I'll call her Frederica. She flew onto the missal midway through the consecration prayer at our parish Eucharist. No doubt attracted by the sweet fragrance of wine, this tiny "nuisance" alighted on the margin of the text beside the words "on the night before he died for us, our Lord Jesus Christ took bread. . . ." Frederica stayed, walking quickly along the book, yet never straying onto the printed words. Clearly she was an "edges bug." When she heard the words "whenever you drink it, do this for the remembrance of me," Frederica flew from the page, maybe to receive the now consecrated wine, and I did not see her again. But she has continued to bug me.

What could a fruit fly have to say to me on this day? Why should I pay attention to a minute messenger from the Maker of all creatures great and very small? Standing at the altar on the day, which marked for me twenty-three years of ordained ministry, I encountered an appropriate reminder of my littleness. Frederica was tiny next to the printed text that contained the sacred words of consecration. As a priest of the church, I am called to the awesome task of celebrating "the mysteries of Christ's body and blood," and a fruit fly comes along to say "Remember your littleness."

Further reflection on Frederica's timely insurgence leads to reflection on the meaning of walking at the edges. In the years

before moving to the United States, I felt marginalized by the Church of England where, because I am a woman, my vocation to the priesthood could not be tested. Since that time, I have met many women and men who struggle to find a place of belonging in our places of worship. They walk at the edges and sometimes leave the page altogether because they feel excluded. Maybe that is because those of us who represent the institution sometimes make ourselves too big. Maybe in our desire for power, we squash the fruit flies.

In the gospels Jesus sees in his own followers the need for a lesson in littleness:

> *An argument arose among them as to which of them was the greatest. But Jesus, aware of their inner thoughts, took a little child and put it by his side, and said to them, "Whoever welcomes this child in my name welcomes me, and whoever welcomes me welcomes the one who sent me; for the least among all of you is the greatest." (Luke 9:46–48)*

Later in the same gospel Jesus blesses children and then says, "Truly I tell you, whoever does not receive the kingdom of God as a little child will never enter it" (Luke 18:17).

In the time of Jesus, children had no voice and no power. They were among God's *anwim*—the poor, sick, women, and all disenfranchised people who deserved protection by the community. They were the "little people" so easily trampled upon and overlooked by those who were power hungry. The margins of the missal represented a challenge for me to remember the easily forgotten people who dwell at the extreme edges of the world, edges where powerlessness and economic oppression imprison them. Recently, I walked the dusty streets of Soweto on the edge of Johannesburg, South Africa, where many people live in tin and cardboard shacks, and a whole street shares a single chemical toilet. I visited men dying in a hospital for AIDS patients—there was no hospital for women victims—where overworked staff offered compassion but had no drugs to ease suffering. And at a kindergarten in a township outside Pretoria, I was present when the children, many of them orphans, received lunchtime bowls of rice, their only meal of the day. I found that my experience as a person of power and privilege in the Third World had the effect of cutting me down to size. I was challenged to prayerfully consider how my lifestyle diminishes others and the ways God asks me to respond with care for the *anwim*.

But Frederica had a great deal more to say about life and ministry here at home. There are hungry and abused children who live in the mountains of western North Carolina; homeless people wander the streets of Asheville; single mothers struggle to support their children on welfare checks; and women's shelters overflow with refuge seekers. How will I respond to these "little people"? Sometimes I identify with the priest and the Levite in the story Jesus told about the Good Samaritan. They were so wrapped up in their bigness that the injured ones along the way were easily passed by. The Church is in the midst of a time of change as it reevaluates the way it interprets the Gospel in a pluralistic world. There are many who feel threatened by changes, and who are afraid that dearly held beliefs will be lost. They are angry with those who advocate new understanding of Scripture in light of scientific, medical, and literary discovery. But others believe that new ways for gospel-living are essential if the church is to survive, and regard more traditional Christians as hopelessly naive. Name calling develops, sides are chosen, the arguments grow, and the poor are forgotten.

A tiny fruit fly came along to remind me that at the heart of the Christian faith lies an invitation to share the feast that unites. We all come as needy, sinful people, opening our hearts and hands to receive Christ again and again in the Eucharistic celebration. But that is not the end of it. We conclude our worship with the prayer: "Send us now into the world in peace, and grant us strength and courage to love and serve you with gladness and singleness of heart; through Christ our Lord. Amen." We are sent out to the edges, to be good news to the little people who need our love. And we can only serve in this way when we become small enough to see and hear Christ in the midst of life, in the pain and joy, needs and giftedness of others, even those with whom we disagree.

REFLECTING WITH SCRIPTURE
Luke 18:9–14
Do arguments about doctrine and practice in your church so engage members that there is little energy left for mission and reaching out to the poor? Are newcomers welcomed into your community? How do you receive God's *anwim*?

PRAYER
God of littleness, show me when I become too big for my own boots. Help me step outside my safety zone to meet those at the margins and to find you there. When I am sure that I am right, remind me to listen to those with whom I disagree so that I may respect and honor each person in the knowledge that we are one in you. Amen.

Discipline

Desirable Realty

The male weaver bird is a tireless builder. In order to construct a nest in which his mate can lay her eggs, he gathers twigs, grasses, and leaves in his beak, flying back and forth to craft a safe nest-globe home with a tiny entrance. The female waits and watches until he is done, then inspects the nest. If it does not satisfy her standard of excellence, she ruthlessly destroys the structure and her spouse must begin again. Mister weaver bird does not give up easily, and he may have to build several nests, which he anchors to a tree limb where they swing like Christmas tree ornaments as the wind blows.

On a visit to Johannesburg, South Africa, I marveled at these elegantly constructed baubles hung on a single tree in the tiny walled garden of friends. By nature I am not a very patient person, and my sympathies were with the poor male bird, building and rebuilding for a fussy, perfectionist spouse. He seemed to be doing his best and was no doubt anxious to get on with the business of creating a family. I watched the female, inwardly criticizing her for her selfish rejection of several "homes," and I wondered what constituted a satisfactory dwelling for her. Slowly my criticism was challenged. Suppose her purpose in destroying some nests was due to her insistence on the safest, strongest possible place in which to rear her offspring? Is it possible that she would accept only a structure that

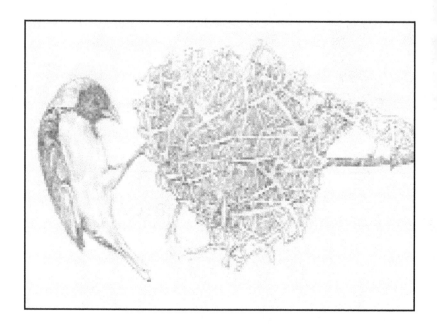

would last through the strong winds and lashing rain that sometimes battered the city and its environment?

The well-known Gospel story of the two builders came to mind as I continued to reflect on the weaver bird. Jesus invited his hearers to pay close attention to where they build and to choose a firm foundation (Matthew 7:24–27). The hard work of constructing a house on a solid rock foundation paid off when storms and floods assaulted the building, but the house built on sandy soil collapsed. The foundation mattered. There is a parallel between the teaching of Jesus and the demand for high standards of construction on the part of the female weaver bird. The initial shaping of the nest with sturdy materials is essential, and no manner of attractive weaving can substitute for the initial "foundation." Brittle twigs and old crumbling leaves do not make a safe and solid nest. Jesus contrasts the wise and foolish builders and, through the parable, challenges us still to consider the foundation and structure of our lives.

Spiritual disciplines, like the discipline of rebuilding that nest, are not always welcomed, but they form the structure which we can continue to build on the Christ-Foundation. The idea of a "Rule of Life" may sound like a rigid formula that quenches the freedom of the Spirit, yet it provides a clear plan for the inner home of our being, where a supportive structure allows for individual growth. In origin, the word "rule" implied a trellis, and I find this concept more inviting than "rule." Several plants may be rooted beside a trellis, but in their uniqueness they move in different directions while remaining attached to the structure. Their diversity adds to the beauty of the whole. I have discovered that there are many blessings associated with a trellis of spiritual disciplines, not least of which is moving beyond wishful thinking about how to follow Christ and choosing instead to be intentional about my discipleship.

For many years I had a Rule of Life provided by a monastic community. As an Associate of the Order, I was required to observe a number of disciplines of prayer, worship, stewardship, study of Scripture, and the sacraments. It was a good beginning and one that helped me to appreciate the value of a personal spiritual discipline lived in connection with the community through regular review and reporting. More recently, I have become part of an ecumenically diverse Covenant group. (By Covenant group I mean that each of us has entered into an agreement to pray for, serve, and support one another.) Our challenge has been to create a trellis that is flexible enough to allow for different vocations, work, and family life and, at the same time, to hold us all together. We have adopted six headings, which we each use to build our personal trellis:

1. Stability—desiring a life of balance and simplicity, we commit to regular prayer, worship, study, and service.
2. Conversion—openness to the grace of God calling us to an ongoing process of change as we attend to the inner rhythms of our lives and seek freedom from encumbering forces that limit encounters with the Holy.
3. Obedience—willingness to listen in order to discern and respond to God's voice revealed through Scripture, creation, and relationships.
4. Recreation—sharing the joy and celebration of our Creator through the renewal of body, mind, and spirit by means of

play, humor, focused energy, passion, and relaxation.

5. Stewardship—rejoicing in God's abundance in order to embrace wise and faithful management of time, money, our bodies, and creation.

6. Action—taking responsibility for compassionate action through service, social justice, peacemaking, prophetic action, and spiritual disciplines.

These building blocks may prove useful in the development of your own structure that rests firmly on the rock foundation of Christ.

The female weaver bird was unwilling to accept substandard housing for her chicks. Her mate wanted to get the job done and move on. I later learned that he is notoriously unfaithful and quickly selects new partners who must begin the nest-building process all over again. No trellis for him; he simply chooses busy activity over faithfulness and care for his spouse and offspring. In the western world, where instant gratification is offered by advertisers, programmers, and spiritual gurus, we may be tempted to sample the religious smorgasbord that requires no investment of time and discipline, offering only a series of spiritual "highs" that cannot sustain us in times of drought or storm. Jesus and the mother weaver bird know better.

REFLECTING WITH SCRIPTURE
1 Corinthians 3:10–17
If you already have a Rule of Life (Trellis), use this passage to review it, and name your building materials. You may also choose to use Paul's instructions and/or the earlier six headings for creating a trellis for the first time.

PRAYER
Loving Creator, for the gift of weaver birds and their wisdom, I offer thanks. Strengthen my resolve to build with the spiritual disciplines that keep me faithful to Christ, the Living Foundation of my faith. May I always be dissatisfied with anything less than the best and always be aware of the grace to begin anew. Amen.

WILDNESS

God Is Not Tame

We spent the morning bumping along unpaved roads in the Lion and Rhino park, stopping frequently to observe animals of the South African veldt in their natural habitat. Many species of buck shyly appeared, including several springbok who bounced gracefully across the landscape. Beside a small creek, several warthogs wallowed in thick mud; ostriches stood bunched together, their nodding heads at the end of long necks suggesting an important meeting was in progress. And a rhino stood motionless on a patch of dry, cracked mud. At one point, we stopped to observe a cheetah, barely visible in the long grass, and later found ourselves surrounded by wild dogs competing for a rodent that one of them had unearthed. Zebra, small lion groups close to the road, buffalo, and a mostly submerged hippo delighted us as we progressed toward a fenced area where we could eat lunch.

We sat at wooden tables waiting for our food to be served, and still the animal population kept us aware that we were in their habitat. A young motherless buck had become so tame she had to be chased away from the dining area several times. Many species of birds observed us as they waited for handouts, and a baby zebra stood in the shade of a thorn tree. He would later accompany us around the enclosure where we could observe a variety of animals

who were part of a breeding program. The game warden had told our group that the park was raising lions for the larger game reserves throughout South Africa, and following lunch, we could visit with some of the babies. Somehow I missed the departure of the group, so I attempted, with one fellow traveler, to find my way to the three-month-old lion cubs.

Outside an enclosure with tall fences we were asked to sign a waiver—I didn't pause long enough to read it—and then allowed to progress into the fenced area. To the right of the gate, a lioness rested, and my first response was to treat her like one of my cats by stooping down to touch her. I quickly learned that this was NOT appropriate behavior with wild cats, who tend to think of anything that moves close to the ground as a potential meal. We moved into the center of the enclosure where her siblings stood—a second lioness and a handsome male—together with a couple of other visitors. I felt awed to be so close to these beautiful wild creatures and moved closer to the female, who seemed to be growing a little restless. In the next moment she approached me, stood on her hind legs, and placed both of her big paws on my shoulders. I stood eye to eye, teeth to teeth, with a powerful lioness whose weight could easily have knocked me to the ground. And I was not afraid. Foolish, perhaps, awed but unafraid. Instinctively, I raised my hand behind my back and placed it on her head, gently pushing her to the ground, much to the relief of the game warden, who decided it was time for visitors to leave. The male had gotten bored and now sat on a large block of concrete about four feet above the ground. I was able to reach out and touch his rear end before we left; I was not about to risk the teeth.

Not until we left the enclosure did I discover that this was not what our guide had in mind when she said that we could play with lions. A second enclosure revealed several cubs, three-months-old, playing like any kittens with human assistance. This was where we were supposed to go. The lions I had encountered were adolescents, ten-months-old, almost full grown and ready shortly to be transferred to a larger reserve where they would need to fend for themselves. The lions had been bred in the park and, from the beginning, had encountered humans. But they remained wild animals. These lions were not tame and, blessedly, never would be.

My encounter with the lioness caused me to ponder the wonder of wildness. I recalled the stories of the lion Aslan in *The Lion, the Witch and the Wardrobe*. When the children first hear about the lion who will liberate snowbound Narnia, Susan asks: "Is he quite safe? I shall feel rather nervous about meeting a lion." Mr. Beaver, one of the brave animals who dared to defy the White Witch by joining an underground rebellion that will return Narnia to Aslan, its rightful leader, replies: "Who said anything about safe? 'Course he isn't safe.

But he's good. He's the King, I tell you."[2] Aslan is absolutely not a
tame lion, but he is a profoundly loving Creature. In the Narnia
stories, Aslan represents the power of good, the Christ, who brings
new hope to the land that has been locked in fear by the evil White
Witch who has created perpetual winter. This story is as old as
humanity itself in its central message of the struggle between good
and evil, and the cost of aligning oneself with the Creator whose
purpose is freedom and harmony between all creatures. It also pres-
ents us with a question: Which side are you on? Are you willing to
stand firm, in the presence of raw divinity, and confront the Enemy
of peace and compassion?

Those who encounter the wildness of God are changed by
the experience. And the encounters come in many other ways
besides meetings with lions. The fugitive Moses was first overcome
in the presence of the Holy One through a bush blazing with fire in
the desert. Moses approached because he noticed that, despite the
flames, the bush was not consumed. He quickly realized his vulnerability as he stood before this unprecedented, and apparently unending, fire: "Come no closer! Remove the sandals from your feet, for
the place on which you are standing is holy ground. . . . and Moses
hid his face because he was afraid to look at God" (Exodus 3:5–6).
The God of Lions and burning bushes is not tame, but is very, very
good.

REFLECTING WITH SCRIPTURE
Matthew 14:22–33
Can you recall moments in your life when you have been confronted by the wildness of God? In what ways do we try to "tame" God
today?

PRAYER
Creator of all things, present in mountains and anthills, crashing
waves and trickling streams, we honor your wildness. We see you in

---

2. C. S. Lewis, *The Lion, the Witch and the Wardrobe* (New York:
    HarperCollins, 1950), 80.

the great elephant who moves silently through a forest and in the mole who spoils our carefully manicured lawn. You are present in the great cats that hunt and in their prey who run and die. You come to us sometimes gentle as a mother suckling her child but also as Fire, Wind, and Earthquake to arrest our attention. Show us the deceptions we engage in to keep you at a safe distance and give us the courage to approach with awe and trust in your consuming love. Amen.

HABITAT

The Three Bears—and Momma

One evening in late summer, my elderly cat Bonnie came flying though her cat door. She had been resting on the screen porch, her favorite place of observation, but now her ears were set back and her eyes were wild as she ran into the house. A dog in the yard, I thought to myself, or maybe a neighborhood cat come to taunt her captivity. I casually looked out the window and, sure enough, there was a furry black shape near the bird feeder. I was about to bang on the window to shoo the "dog" away when she stood on hind legs by the feeder and with a heart-pounding shock, I saw that my visitor was a black bear.

I live in the mountains of North Carolina—bear country—but this was my first close encounter with one of these creatures whose habitat I had invaded. It was an awesome moment. I soon saw that she was not alone; playing on the mossy earth beside her were three cubs, a few months old and just as endearing as the picture post cards we sell to visitors who crowd our small town in the fall. I had no idea what to do on finding myself so close to black bears intent on destroying my carefully constructed bird feeders. Naively I called the police department for advice and was told, "Stay inside until they go away, Ma'am."

Despite the officer's advice, I did open the door just a crack and

banged on a copper pan when the mother bear began to bend a
wrought iron bird feeder until it was level to the ground. She simply
stood and hissed at me while her cubs climbed the nearest tree. They
spent the rest of the evening peeking around the tree trunk. I left my
post by the window and telephoned several friends to impress them
with the tale of my bear visitors and also called immediate neighbors
to suggest they might want to stay inside also. About fifteen minutes
later, I looked outside once again; the cubs were still in their tree, but
I could see no sign of momma bear. With my face close to the window pane, I scanned the yard and suddenly there she was, stretching
her big paw and face toward the thistle seed feeder suspended next

to the glass. We were separated by about six inches and a thin pane of glass. I recalled Henry David Thoreau's experience as he sat in his cabin at Walden Pond and became aware of role reversal. He was now the observed one within the "cage" of his own construction.

The woods that surround my house have been home to bears and many other wild creatures for centuries. Our small neighborhood was developed in their habitat, and it is natural for them to return when berries and other food sources become scarce at higher elevations. Besides, bird food offers a quick and easy meal, especially for a lactating female with other mouths to feed. I was honored to have them on the property that I inappropriately call mine. And they had a lesson to teach me: Habitat is important. Knowing where we belong keeps us aware of the choices we must make to keep on the pilgrim way toward home. The author of the Epistle to the Hebrews underscores this point when he writes of Abraham who, as he journeyed by faith, "looked forward to the city that has foundations, whose architect and builder is God" (Hebrews 11:10). Two chapters later he applies this to Christians: "Here we have no lasting city, but we are looking for the city that is to come" (Hebrews 13:14).

A few of us have lived in the same area, even the same house, for a lifetime. Most of us have moved many times as college, marriage, or occupation determined where we needed to settle. But as people of faith, we are aware that we live in two zones—our physical, geographical habitat and the realm of God, our true home. We can perhaps understand this if we think about two circles that interconnect, forming an ellipse in the center. One side of the ellipse represents the world in which we live, the other God's eternal commonwealth, where we truly belong. While we are on earth, we live in the ellipse, fully committed to shape our lives so that we honor the environment in which we dwell but also conscious that our home is with God in "the city which is to come."

From time to time on our faith journey, we are blessed with glimpses of eternity. Like the bears who found bounty in my yard, we are drawn by grace into moments of celebration with God. A veil is lifted and we see the holy, feel divine presence, and sense that we stand on the threshold of promise. Celtic Christians made little distinction between this world and the world that is to come, so they lived with a deep awareness of the presence of the Creator in all things. They also believed that those who had gone ahead on life's pilgrimage were living presences and their prayers reflect the sense that support was found through the communion of saints. In the nineteenth century, George MacLeod described the island of Iona off the coast of western Scotland as a "thin place," suggesting that the membrane between this life and life beyond death was almost permeable there. Living consciously in the ellipse, we discover many such places in our experience, and they help us to keep journeying toward our true habitat.

REFLECTING WITH SCRIPTURE
Psalm 90:1–2
What does it mean to you to believe that God is your dwelling place? When do you feel most "at home" with the Creator?

PRAYER
Loving Creator, you are our true home and Guide along the way. Keep us always returning to you, the Source of our life, when we find ourselves in a far country. Help us, day by day, to be still with you, resting in the hospitality of grace where we are always at home. Amen.

DANCE

High Wire Act

I am blessed by mornings. The miracle of dawn is a sign of hope and newness and an invitation to walk with God into a fresh day, a fresh start. All too soon, however, the tasks of ordinary everyday living begin to consume me and I forget the early-morning moments of hope. It is often the creatures of God that help me to return to the place of prayerful faith, even the ones we sometimes call "pests." I wrote this poem in 1986 when I lived with a monastic community in the South Carolina low country and saw, through the screen door of my small cabin, a reminder of the holy in the ordinary:

Squirrel on a telephone cable poised
Racing lightly
Along the cobra blackness
you waken me again
to the vibrancy of this new day.

I had forgotten,
so soon after first sight,
the bursting freshness of the morning

for inner dialogue,
the rehearsal of old fears,
robbed me of the moment.

Then you made your entrance,
interrupting the tired drama
with dancing abandon.
I am graced by your coming
drawn back into the cosmic spiral of joy.

In the liturgical calendar we sometimes speak of "ordinary time," referring to those seasons of the year outside Advent, Christmas, Epiphany, Easter, and Pentecost. Ordinary time is a reminder that much of our spiritual experience unfolds in ways and times that are not spectacular. But in another sense, there is no such thing as ordinary time, for each moment is filled with the possibility of discovering God's hidden presence. Practicing awareness helps us to break through the numbing busyness of our lives into "the sacrament of the present moment," a phrase coined by the seventeenth-century Jesuit writer Jean Pierre de Caussade. When awareness gets eroded by daily chores and demanding work, God sometimes sends along a reminder of grace in the body of an animal-angel. So it is important to look out of the window from time to time.

Squirrels are common creatures, numerous and death-defying on our roads, robbers in our yards. They are masters at overcoming any challenge, and I have yet to find a bird feeder that is totally squirrel-proof. Squirrels are also wonderful entertainers who remind us that we need to "lighten up" and join in the dance of joy with the Creator. They chase and chatter at each other, leaping onto the thinnest of branches as they plunge and rocket through the trees. Ingenious thieves, they perform athletic break-ins, even overcoming petroleum jelly–covered greasy poles that support bird feeders. Squirrels cause cats to be demented and dogs to bark in frustrated irritation as they play "catch me if you can" around the yard. And squirrels wait for us to notice them too.

On the morning I wrote that poem, I had gotten so busy with the demands of the day that I had forgotten how blessed I had been by dawn as the cicadas began their daily chorus and the birds woke up. Anxiety had become my companion. I looked at all there was to do, thinking that I needed to just keep going if I were to complete even a fraction of the tasks that awaited my attention. Living in a monastery does not mean that there is all the time in the world to smile benignly and stay in church for long hours. The monks and I had most of the everyday chores and responsibilities that we all face. Trash had to be hauled to the dump; meals cooked; the house cleaned; bills paid; and the property maintained. Since we functioned as a retreat center, there were also many administrative tasks, and those who came there on retreat often needed time with us as they looked for help on their spiritual journey. Sometimes we might have to call the local farmer when his bull strayed again onto the site and guests fled, terrified, to their cabins, or undertake a snake rescue when one of the footpaths provided a sunbathed herpetological haven. All these tasks might distract or overwhelm us, but they might also become blessed interruptions that refocused us on the Holy One who meets us at the beginning of each new day.

Squirrels don't wait shyly for you to notice them; they are demanding and always hungry. Their kamikaze leaps through the trees proclaim that there are no ordinary days, only days in which to celebrate, dance, let go, and remember—remember the God of dawn who is also God of the working day to whom our gratitude belongs.

Reflecting with Scripture
Mark 1:35–39
Do you live in a city or work in a place where there are few or no windows? Consider making a small "altar" with plants and natural objects that remind you of the Creator. Pray for the grace to allow these reminders of God's love to dance into your gaze from time to time during the day.

Prayer
New every morning is your love, O God of life, and all day you are with us through busy times and forgetfulness. Send us reminders of your grace when our hope wanes and we become overwhelmed by the many demands on our energy. Restore us to lightness of heart and lead us in the dance of unending joy. Amen.

ANGER

Snap Judgments

Jaws is a black Lurcher with one eye. When I first met him, he attempted to make a meal out of me and was barely restrained by his adoptive owner. His early life is a mystery, though it almost certainly was marked by abuse. Jaws was blessed with two eyes when he came from the shelter, but a run-in with Meg, a large tortoiseshell feline (also an adoptee) deprived him of his right eye. His name is really Solo, but his long pointed nose and abundant supply of teeth earned him the nickname Jaws.

I have grown respectfully fond of Jaws over the months since I first met him. These days, he will sometimes leap onto the armchair where I sit, long skinny legs tangled beneath him and long tongue attempting to lick any part of my skin available to him. Jaws will gently take my arm into his mouth in a gesture I have learned to recognize as an invitation to play. We tussle together until one of us is exhausted—usually me. Jaws remains a ferocious watchdog who means business when he is on the attack, but beneath the bravado is a playful faithfulness toward those he has learned to trust.

Jaws reminds me that in many human relationships, gruffness, and sometimes downright attack, may mask a deep longing to be loved and set free from fear. When someone "snaps" at me, my first reaction is to retaliate, fight back, and retort in a way designed to

hurt. I don't ask, at least in the beginning, why this person is being angry and hurtful. There could be many reasons why the "snapper" chooses an attack mode—maybe insensitive words spoken by someone else are brought to mind by something I have now said, or maybe physical or psychological pain; or maybe it's just self-protection stemming from a history of abuse. It took a while for Jaws to trust me, and for a while I needed to let him bark and snarl until he was satisfied that I did not intend to hurt him.

When Paul wrote to Christians in the province of Galatia, he reminded them of the central command of Jesus that they are to love one another. "The whole law is summed up in a single command-ment, 'You shall love your neighbor as yourself.' If, however, you bite and devour one another, take care that you are not consumed by one another. Live by the Spirit . . ." (Galatians 5:14–16). In the church-es that Paul served, there were differences of opinion, diverse practices, and, sometimes, a party spirit that destroyed unity. Various groups thought they were right and that any who did not agree with them were clearly wrong. In some cases wrangling threatened to destroy the church and bring shame on its members when disputes became public. This kind of behavior was a denial of the Gospel and clear evidence that Christians did not have "the mind of Christ" (Philippians 2:5). Snap judgments, made about others who appear to be on the attack, are rarely accurate. Living with the differences, listening to those who disagree with us, and approaching them with patience and love allows them to move a little closer toward trust and to find healing.

Struggles with differences in doctrine and practice are very much alive in our churches today. Frequently, the debates that take place are more focused on scoring points than understanding the opposition and prayerfully moving toward consensus. Sometimes irreconcilable differences lead to a parting of the ways, but when this happens, grace asks us to forgive and to go on loving our "enemies." I have stopped reading letters to the editor in the weekly publication of my own denomination; in the climate of current debate over human sexuality, so many correspondents on both sides seem intent on vilifying others and representing themselves as the sole posses-sors of truth. I am willing to talk with those who desire genuine dialogue, but I find the letters filled with anger wearying, and I can respond best by praying for—rather then reacting to—the writers. I do not wish to use their vitriolic as a means of sharpening my teeth.

Jaws loves to be loved. He has boundless energy and those long, skinny legs carry him far across the fields and footpaths of his native England. He still has a tendency to bite anyone who represents a threat, but if he is allowed to be himself and to play the way dogs love to play, he will accept a new friend with enthusiasm. And the person who chooses to feed and nurture need not fear those sharp, snapping teeth; Jaws will dance and wag his tail in ecstasy in anticipation of any morsel that can satisfy his not-too-discriminating palate.

REFLECTING WITH SCRIPTURE
Philippians 2:5–11
Do you know someone who differs with you and always seems to "push your buttons" when you are together? Consider sending a greeting card to that person, expressing appreciation for who they are and letting them know that you accept and pray for them.

PRAYER
God of unchanging love and patience, help me to see those I find difficult as beautiful people made in your image. Enable me to recognize my own quick and critical responses to others and to care for my own wounds. Help me to celebrate brokenness in the knowledge that you are the Great Healer of all our disease and the Reconciler of all our differences. Amen.

STUCK-NESS

Silly Goose

It is mid-winter on a raw, cold day in the mountains of North Carolina. Wearing boots, a warm coat, scarf, and hat, I venture outdoors and drive to Lake Tomahawk, where the usual gaggle of ducks and geese wait to be fed. Today, the lake is almost completely frozen over. Only at the shallower end, where the birds crowd and cackle together, is there a small opening in the ice. A few walkers have stopped to enjoy the antics of upended ducks, geese battling one another for food, and the ubiquitous pigeons waiting for the grain that does not make it all the way into the water. It is a lively scene, and I notice that several visiting Canada geese have joined the regulars at the lake. I walk briskly along the footpath and encounter another hardy group of joggers gathered at the bank and looking at something in the middle of the lake. A solitary goose sits on the ice, firmly stuck, and unable to free its frozen feet.

To begin with, onlookers call encouragement to the goose and assess the possibility of rescue, but the ice is too thin to safely hold a human savior. Then someone remembers that a row boat is stored at the senior center located at the lower end of the lake, and two young men are dispatched to retrieve it. The boat is lowered into the one remaining area of water, but there is no possibility of rowing, so the oars are used as ice-breakers. Using the blunt end of the oars, the

rescuers pound the ice, laboriously smashing a small portion at a time, and very slowly inching toward the frozen goose. The poor creature is clearly terrified, protesting loudly, but unable to free itself from the ice or the approaching helpers who are, undoubtedly, perceived as a further threat. Finally, the last fragments of ice that imprison the goose are loosened and with a squawk of terror, the silly goose is free. Moments later, it paddles with its siblings, who are still competing for handouts, all of them now behaving as though nothing untoward had happened.

I was an adventurous child and often found myself in places from which I needed rescue. And I recall that, many times, I was called "a silly goose." The expression was used not in anger, but with a resigned acceptance of my waywardness; it suggested endearment rather than judgment. "There you go again! Will you ever learn? You are a silly goose!" It is entirely appropriate to allow children to learn through their explorations of a world full of possibilities—so long as parents or caregivers remain vigilant and ready to do what it takes to bring the child back to safety. We learn by risking, pushing at boundaries, and bumping up against our belief that we are invincible. Inevitably, though, there are times when we find ourselves stuck, vulnerable, and unable to do anything to save ourselves. Then we can only sit, and wait, and squawk in that uncomfortable and humiliating place. We must wait for rescue.

In the Gospels, Peter is frequently represented as a headstrong man whose impetuous nature often landed him in trouble. Peter had a good heart, but he was not always able to live up to his words, and sometimes fear led him into places of defeat and despair. If Jesus had known the expression, he would probably have called Peter a "silly goose." Jesus loved Peter and saw him as a potentially rocklike person, but there were many times in his discipleship when Peter failed, and when he needed rescue from dangerous places. After feeding the five thousand hungry people who had spent the day listening to him, Jesus sends the disciples away by boat, dismisses the crowd, and then goes up into the mountains to pray. Early the next morning, the disciples are stunned to see Jesus approaching them on the water, and they are understandably frightened, thinking that they are seeing a ghost. Jesus reassures them, but Peter isn't too sure that he can believe what he sees: "Lord, if it is you, command me to come to you on the water," and Jesus says, "Come" (Matthew 14:28–29). Peter steps out of the boat and begins to make his way to Jesus, but when he notices the strong wind, he becomes frightened and starts to sink. "Lord save me!" he yells, and Jesus immediately stretches out his hand and helps the terrified disciple back into the boat. Like the silly goose, Peter was rescued from a place of great danger and brought to safety.

The stuck places on our spiritual journey teach us just how much we need God and how ready God is to act when we cry out. Sometimes prayer becomes dull, and boredom sets in. We quit praying and forget about the One who loves us and yearns for us to return home—until something happens to remind us of our need for God to lift us out of the stuck place. With generosity and compassion, God will go to great lengths to come to us where we are, even if it means breaking up the ice-flows of willfulness that have distanced us from the Source of our life. When we are set free, there is a returning not only to God but to the community of God's people as we join together in the feast that is always prepared for us by the loving hands of our Rescuer.

REFLECTING WITH SCRIPTURE
Psalm 40:1–5
Have you ever felt "stuck" on your spiritual journey? Where are you right now? Do you perhaps know someone who needs encouragement to allow God to ease them out of a cold, isolated place?

PRAYER
God of stuck places, thank you for always being there when we are frozen in our waywardness. Keep us aware of your love and compassion and help us to be patient with ourselves in our silliness. Give us grace to see the humor in our foolishness so that we do not take ourselves too seriously. Amen.

COMPASSION

Gentle Giants

During an evening drive through the Kwa Maritane game reserve in Gauteng Province, South Africa, we encountered a large herd of elephants, including several babies. The elephants emerged from a group of trees and slowly crossed the unpaved, dusty road ahead of us. They made little sound as they traveled toward a water hole where other animals were already gathered. After they passed, we moved slowly forward, unaware that several more elephants were still sheltered by the trees. Then a large bull spotted us; he was not happy. Several more little ones began to cross the road with two females, and the bull spread his ears, raised his trunk, and trumpeted a warning. We readily acknowledged our intrusion, respecting the elephants' claim on their habitat, and waited with awe as the stragglers crossed the road to join the rest of the herd.

The following morning, I waited in an underground hide where barred openings allowed visitors to observe at eye level another water hole that offered close viewing of animals without their awareness of human presence. They came to drink in orderly sequence: birds, buck, baboons, zebra, and then a single, large male elephant. He lumbered to the edge of the pool and drank deeply before throwing water back over his body through his trunk. Then he began to circle the pool, and I found myself a few inches away

from his large foot and could hear deep breathing as his highly sensitive trunk vacuumed the ground. He went on his way to the far side of the pool where he settled down for a dust bath until his body was covered with clouds of dry, sandy soil. He seemed to thoroughly enjoy this playful activity, and I watched until he got up and made his way back through the brush and trees, tail swinging between his great hips.

Elephants live and travel in family groups and care deeply for one another. The young are protected by the mother and several "aunts," and the bulls will charge at anything that threatens their offspring. Elephants mourn the loss of one of their own in a way that is akin to human grieving, gathering round the corpse and keeping watch. They have burial grounds and seem to sense when they are close to death, making their way to one of these sites. Hunters learned that a bereaved elephant would often visit the burial place of a spouse to grieve, and they used this knowledge to track and kill big "tuskers" for their ivory. With few nonhuman predators, elephants survive well in their natural habitat and provide a wonderful example of compassionate care for one another. In our time, when we frequently speak of dysfunctional families, we might learn a lot by paying attention to the wisdom of our elephant brothers and sisters.

In the Gospel according to John, we find the only account of Jesus washing the disciples feet. Jesus assumes the role of a servant by stooping to this menial task, and it causes the disciples great embarrassment as their Teacher kneels before them. "Do you know what I have done for you?" Jesus asks when he has finished the foot washing; he goes on to say: "You call me Teacher and Lord—and you are right, for that is who I am. So, if I, your Lord and Teacher, have washed you feet, you also ought to wash one another's feet. For I have set you an example" (John 13:12–15). In the chapters that follow, Jesus repeats again and again that the disciples are to love one another as he has loved them—they are to become family for one another. Love and compassion are the keynotes of Christian discipleship.

Our biological families are not always harmonious. Gatherings for anniversaries, birthdays, or public holidays are frequently marked by dissension and rivalry. If we are to function well, we need to grow beyond our differences and learn to appreciate diversity rather than wasting energy trying to prove we are better, or that our perspective is the only right one. The same is true of the Christian family. The many different denominations that exist in Christendom bear witness to difference, and historically we know that many of them were formed because brothers and sisters could not agree on some issue of faith or practice. Jesus never says to the disciples, "Make sure you agree with each other." Instead he says, "Love one another"

(John 15:12). When love is our guiding principle, we can be together as family, protecting young and sick family members, grieving
with the dying, and honoring the lives of those who have gone
before. Instead of defending our dearly held opinions, we can open
our ears and hearts to those with whom we disagree and assure them
that they are also loved and valued in the family of God.

From my observation of elephants, I believe they know how to
enjoy life, how to play. Perhaps the answer to our all-too-serious
attempts to prove ourselves right would become less important if we
learned how to laugh at ourselves a little and engage in playfulness
with each other. What might be the equivalent for us of a good dust
bath or a romp through the veldt? One of the most joyful celebrations of diversity I have ever known took place as more than three
hundred delegates of the first Global Summit of United Religions
Initiative joined local worshipers in a march along the beach front
in Rio de Janeiro. This was no solemn walk. We sang together, while
some danced, others played instruments and chanted, and all of us
exchanged greetings with surprised Sunday beach goers. If anyone
had asked about belief systems we held dear, the responses would
have been vastly different, yet we had discovered a deep connection
with one another in our desire to engage in peace-building. That day
we all believed that we will see an end to violence, inequity, and
oppression only when we recognize that we are family, that we
belong to the global village we call earth, and that love and not
hatred is what joins us.

Back at Kwa Maritane a year later, we again entered the game
reserve through one of the lodges and had traveled only a short
distance when we came upon a long line of vehicles and had to stop.
Shortly after we arrived, the cars began backing up and we all had to
reverse slowly, those of us at the end wondering what was happening up ahead. It turned out that a very angry bull elephant had taken
exception to visitors approaching too close to the family he guarded,
and was preparing to charge at the closest vehicle. Fortunately, as we
all backed up, he changed his mind and by the time our car arrived
at the spot, all we saw was the bulk of his form disappearing into the
trees. Maybe this was the same elephant I saw flinging dust over
himself, playing by the water hole. Maybe I can be fiercely protec-

tive of the family of God, willing to confront potential destroyers, without forgetting to celebrate the life I have been given.

REFLECTING WITH SCRIPTURE
Colossians 3:12–17
Where do you see compassionate caring in today's world? How does your church or community provide protection for the young and needy, and enable each person to feel that they are part of the family?

PRAYER
Great God, Father and Mother of us all, in your compassion you encircle us in times of danger and nurture us with your love. Help us to share your care for all your family so that no one is forgotten and no one is abandoned when they need encouragement. May we learn through playfulness to join you in celebration of all creation as "very good." Amen.

FEAR

Tail of a Scaredy Cat

Bede is an orange tabby scaredy cat. We met when I went to the shelter looking for two cats, preferably siblings, who had outgrown the exhausting kitten stage. When I called the shelter staff, I learned that they were caring for two cats who seemed to fit my description, and since older cats were difficult to place, I was just the kind of adoptive human they longed to hear from. The following Sunday afternoon I visited a large local pet store where animals from two area shelters were taken each week to await adoption. I was introduced to the two cats we had spoken about, but couldn't resist looking at all the others. The antics of numerous kittens and the longing eyes of older animals were captivating. I stood watching, wanting to take them all home, and now needing to make a decision. Then I felt a gentle touch on my knee. Looking down, I saw an orange paw thrust through the bars of a cage and knew that I had found my housemates. These were not the two cats I had expected to take home with me, but Bede seduced me with a paw touch and hopeful, hazel eyes. Bede and his sister Brigid were between nine months and a year old, and she had already had a litter of kittens. I signed the adoption papers for them, and they traveled the twenty miles to my house crowded in a single cat carrier.

For the first few days, I kept the cats in my bedroom, allowing

them to become comfortable with a small space before freeing them
to explore the whole house. Bede climbed the pillows on my bed and
sat regally looking down. He had been named Coriander, but his
posture suggested "the Venerable Bede," a monk and scholar of the
eighth-century CE from my native England. Bede became
Coriander's official name when he went to the vet for his first check-
up and shots. As I write, Bede is attempting to join me at my desk;

he still demands attention with a paw pat, and he has a great need to be close to me.

Bede is afraid of strangers and loud noises, especially the vacuum cleaner. He and his sister Brigid spend a lot of time out on the screened porch where they can watch—and talk to—the squirrels and birds who come tantalizingly close to the mesh, but there is trouble if another feline dares to enter the yard. Bede sets up a caterwaul and his long, slim tail becomes a bottle brush. It is not a good idea to touch Bede when he is in this agitated state, as I discovered to my cost when I reached out to reassure him one time and received a deep puncture wound as his claws met my hand. He had not meant to hurt me, but fear and agitation robbed him of control. Bede needs frequent affirmation, loves to be petted, and finds ingenious hiding places when he is afraid, which is often.

There are many places in Scripture where "Do not be afraid" is spoken to God's people. Like Bede, we need to be reassured that we are loved, and the love of God we long for is mostly manifested through human companions. Isaiah is the spokesman conveying God's words of reassurance to ancient Israel: "Do not fear; for I have redeemed you; I have called you by name, you are mine" (Isaiah 43:1). Mary hears reassurance from the messenger Gabriel when she reacts in terror to his presence: "Do not be afraid, Mary, for you have found favor with God" (Luke 1:30). What Gabriel goes on to say is incomprehensible, frightening, and ultimately life-changing; Mary needs to be told that this is of God, who loves and chooses her. The disciples caught in a scary wind storm on Galilee wake Jesus from his nap, saying, "Lord, save us!" to which Jesus replies: "'Why are you afraid, you of little faith?' Then he got up and rebuked the winds and the sea; and there was a dead calm" (Matthew 8:25–26).

Bede finds big storms everywhere. The UPS truck rolling over my graveled yard, and the delivery person on the doorstep strike terror into him: "Bede, why are you afraid? I am here with you, I won't let you get hurt." Friends arrive with their noisy children, and Bede flees into the basement: "It's okay, Bede; they are not going to hurt you, and I am here to take care of you. And that predatory neighborhood cat who sometimes comes into the yard does not belong as you do; he cannot do us harm; you are still top cat and I love you."

I have no idea what fears may have found a lodging in Bede due to his experience before I knew him. I do know that my own fears are often irrational, and my defensiveness is triggered by memories of verbal abuse, failure, and taunting by others. But the memories come from within, making me tense, putting me in attack mode—it is not safe to be around me, since I may lash out. But when I stop and recognize the fear for what it is, I hear the echo of Jesus' words: "Why are you afraid?" God walks with us in the events of our lives when fear threatens to take over and we need once more to hear Jesus say, "Peace! Be still!" The enemies on our faith journey, both real and imagined, lose their power when we look them in the face and claim the peaceful presence of Christ.

A long orange tail reveals Bede's presence as he hides beneath the bed. This time, though, he is waiting to pounce on his sister and to initiate their daily, wild chase through the house. They scare each other as they hide behind doors, leap from tables, and race up and down the stairs. This is fun scariness. Play is one of the ways that creative energy is unleashed and a sense of equilibrium restored. The cats remind me that I need to play, relax, have fun, and refuse to be fettered by fear. They help me to remember to stop my intense worrying about the things I do not understand and cannot fix, the stormy passages I have to navigate, and the deeply ingrained fear of old "enemies." It's time to stop chasing my tail and to allow the gift of humor to lift me out of old routines into lighthearted playful joy in God.

REFLECTING WITH SCRIPTURE
Luke 12:22–32
What do you worry about? Are there ways in which you could become more aware of the presence of God on your daily journey? How will you play?

PRAYER
God of peace, you calm the storms of life and invite us into trust. Help us to remember you when fear threatens to rob us of joy on the journey. Give us playful hope in your ever-present love so that we may celebrate the goodness of all we encounter day by day. Amen.

PLAY

Now You See Them, Now You Don't

We humans are sometimes so goal-oriented and driven that we forget to play. Even our games are turned into competitions with winners and losers and are played with great seriousness. Small children and animals know better. There is great delight in watching babies as they learn to observe their new world and begin to play with rattles, suspended toys, and even their own toes. The young of other animal species learn survival skills through playful chasing of one another, and they create "toys" from items at hand in the natural world. Young puppies entertain us with their boundless energy as they race around the yard, play tug-of-war with an old rope, tumble in the grass, and growl fiercely at their kin who try to claim a ball or frisby. Animals are wise enough to continue their playfulness well into adulthood instead of becoming serious and forgetful of the joys of recreation. My two adult cats love to hide beneath the bed skirt and spring out at one another to initiate wild chases throughout the house, and they are always ready to respond to my invitation to catch one of their toy mice.

In the Arizona desert, prairie dogs offer endless entertainment. They live in warrens below ground and appear from holes scattered over the landscape only to disappear and, a moment later, emerge again from a different "doorway." Prairie dogs are territorial, and

they become very excited if they sense intruders close by. The look-out chatters and dances up and down, sometimes somersaulting backwards in a hilarious display of self-importance. Meanwhile, the younger prairie dogs seem never still; they scamper and play hide-and-seek over the dry earth, round rocks and vegetation, in and out of the burrows. I never tire of watching the antics of these playful creatures who make me laugh and help remind me that work is not all there is. I need to relax, reclaim a sense of humor, and engage in some fun from time to time.

Sometimes I like to engage in fantasy as I read certain biblical narratives. Have you ever imagined the scene as God created the world and all the creatures in it? I think God must have been a bit like a child with some clay, fashioning the most amazing beasts, chuckling as humps were put on camels, the giraffe's neck stretched, and big cats adorned with stripes or spots. Then there were the kangaroos and all those other marsupials who were given a ready-made pocket in which to carry their young, raccoons with two back eyes, and scaly dinosaurs who ran and flew over the earth. And what about Noah's ark? I somehow cannot imagine an orderly line of pairs of each species moving politely like people in the notorious British queue. Did the buffalo butt his head into the rear of the slow-moving hippopotamus, or the monkey claim a ride on the back of the elephant? When they got inside, did each couple retire sedately into their appointed suite or was there some disagreement about who had the best space and biggest porthole? Was Noah's wife kept busy chasing after the ostrich, who loved to run marathons and did not want to be contained in his room? How did she deal with the mice, always underfoot, and the parrot who would let out a screech in the kitchen just as she was pouring Noah's afternoon tea? I don't mean to be irreverent toward the Bible, but I think God wants us to nurture our sense of humor and play a bit.

The prophet Zechariah relates God's promises for a restored Jerusalem, "The streets of the city will be full of boys and girls playing in its streets" (Zechariah 8:5), and Jesus teaches that we all need to become like children if we are to enter the "kingdom of God." When parents were bringing children to Jesus, the disciples tried to push them back, but Jesus said: "'Let the little children come to me; do not stop them; for it is to such as these that the kingdom of God belongs. Truly I tell you, whoever does not receive the kingdom of God as a little child will never enter it.' And he took them up in his arms, laid his hands on them, and blessed them" (Mark 10:14–16). How do little children teach us to become members of God's commonwealth? Children are naturally playful, creative, vulnerable, and trusting. We adults need to be reminded of the power of imagination and play and to know that we are not in control of the world or even of ourselves. We need to live less in our heads, instead allowing our hearts to lead us into the presence and embracing love of God where we are at home and trustful.

A friend of mine tells of her decision one beautiful summer day to drive into the country instead of going to church. She did not go without guilt—after all, she had been raised to faithfully attend Sunday services and church school. At first, she felt even more guilt-ridden as she passed churchgoers on her way out of town, but she was also stuck by how serious and unhappy many of these Sunday worshipers seemed. My friend pulled into a parking lot off the Blue Ridge Parkway and found that several families had already arrived with children and dogs. Games of frisby were under way, and as she and her own dog joined in, she observed the contrast between the church people she had just passed in her car and this fun-loving group. Something is wrong with this picture. I certainly do not encourage Christians to give up regular church attendance, since it is essential to be part of a community of faith to sustain us in our daily life with God, but we do need to give time to play and celebration. We need to "become as children" and to let the little ones teach us how to recover imagination and joy in God's presence.

The Hebrew people celebrated their joy in the worship of Yahweh with dance, and instruments such as the trumpet, lute, harp, tambourine, strings, pipe, and cymbals. Psalms 149 and 150 are songs of praise to God, a joyful celebration of God's presence and grace. This sounds playful to me. During the time I was teaching at a London seminary, I went with a group of students on a mission to Wales. Throughout the week, we lived and worked with parishioners and their children in a city that still lived with the pain of a disastrous coal tip slide that had claimed the lives of many children. We prayed with families, offered a healing ministry, and were given responsibility for the Sunday services. In the morning, the worship was a traditional Eucharistic celebration with well-known hymns and liturgy, but the evening service was different. We had spent time with a group of parishioners reflecting on these two psalms and asking ourselves how we might bring more playfulness and joy into the worship. Out of our discussions, we began to create dance to help us celebrate God's presence through all the changes of our lives, and we used a tambourine or two as accompaniment. Most of the regular members of the church found the experience moving, but one woman got up as soon as the dance began and pushed aside the rector, who was standing near the door at the rear of the church. "I never thought I would live to see the day when there was *dancing* in the Lord's house!" she declared. Clearly she was unfamiliar with Hebrew Scriptures that set a precedent for playful joy in the sanctuary.

REFLECTING WITH SCRIPTURE
Jeremiah 31:1–6

How does play and humor find a place in your spiritual life? Are there ways in which you might invite others into a more playful delight in God?

PRAYER

Lord of the dance, we celebrate your gifts of laughter and play. Help us to bring joy to all people, revealing to them your invitation to gather with us as children in your loving presence. We ask you to show us when we get too busy and serious to play, and give us the grace to laugh at ourselves when we become too grown-up. Thank you for all the funny animals that make us smile as they reveal your creativity and imagination. Amen.

FLEXIBILITY

Snake Dance

Snakes are despised by many people. Perhaps the story of Eve and the serpent in Genesis 3 is responsible for the association of snakes with evil, though it neglects another important biblical story of the healing symbolism of snakes. Some members of the community who journeyed through the wilderness under the leadership of Moses were bitten by snakes after they complained about the hardships they were encountering. This event is interpreted as the judgment of Yahweh. In order to provide healing, "Moses made a serpent of bronze, and put it upon a pole; and whenever a serpent bit someone, that person would look to the serpent of bronze and live" (Numbers 21:9). The snake entwined on a lance has remained a symbol of healing to this day. Snakes can also be our teachers, and they certainly need some admirers, since the first instinct of many people is to kill them.

One afternoon, as I sat on the porch of a small cabin in the South Carolina low country, I heard rustling in the leaves and looked up expecting to see a squirrel or turtle. Instead I saw two king snakes in the process of mating. These animals have beautiful markings, and the movement of their bodies as they looped around each other, disentangled, and then came together again in a different formation was truly beautiful. I watched with awe for almost an

hour, caught up in the dance of ecstasy, amazed at their flexibility. There were a number of different species of snake whose habitat I invaded in South Carolina. The black snake was appreciated because it ate rodents and was quite harmless to humans. Copperheads abounded, again with attractive markings, but we gave them a wide berth since they can inflict a painful bite. If they came too close to the house, we would catch them and take them deep into the woods. The sidewinder was fascinating to watch as it zigzagged across the ground, and many tiny multicolored garter snakes lived on insects near the flower beds.

One afternoon, I was returning home and driving along the unpaved road that led to the house when I saw a rattlesnake stretched across the dusty ground. I did not want to run over it so I stopped, but after some time during which there was no movement, I realized it had already become the victim of a vehicle. I got out of the car to take a closer look and saw why the skins of these animals were much desired for making purses and other adornments. This one was magnificent, and I felt tears prickling behind my eyelids as I looked at the intricate design and subtle colors of this creature. Later I wrote a poem about the encounter:

> *Timber rattlesnake*
> *thickly*
> *spread*
> *over the dust*
> *bold, black and amber*
> *chasuble*
> *encasing*
> *the sacrifice.*

I am well aware that there are many deadly snakes in the world and that a healthy fear of approaching too close is appropriate; I have met some of them, safely encased in laboratories in Australia and elsewhere. But we are also learning that the venom of some of these animals contains properties that are now being used to heal previously incurable human diseases. Even if it is difficult to love or see beauty in the snake, we can at the very least value them for their healing gifts and flexibility.

In a world of calendars, meetings, scheduled events, and the sometimes unreasonable expectations of our employers, what place does flexibility play in daily life? Does one interruption, one unexpected emergency, one failure to meet a deadline throw us into a panic that sharpens our rigidity and determination to do more than is reasonable? How can we develop flexibility in our everyday lives and in our journey of faith when sometimes things do not go the way we want? We are offered many stories in the Gospels that show us how Jesus handled constant interruptions as he went about his healing and teaching ministry. On his way to heal the daughter of a rabbi, a woman with chronic hemorrhaging reaches out to Jesus. She tries to keep her touch at the very edge of his garment secret from those who would consider her unclean, but Jesus senses her presence: "Daughter, your faith has made you well; go in peace, and be healed of your disease" (Mark 5:34). Instead of avoiding encounter with the woman, Jesus stops in his tracks, accepts the interruption, and allows her life to become entwined in his compassion, and the dance of God's healing grace. When parents bring children to Jesus for his blessing, the disciples try to protect him from such "unimportant" demands, but he receives the young ones and uses their presence to teach a lesson on humility (Luke 18:15–17). Again, Jesus creates a beautiful dance of joy between himself and playful little ones who were without rights in the culture.

On the return of his disciples, full of stories about the success of their first mission, Jesus attempts to take them to a quiet spot where he could help them reflect, but it was not to be. A great crowd follows them and, as the day wears on, becomes hungry. "Send the crowd away so that they may go into the surrounding villages and countryside, to lodge and get provisions; for we are here in a deserted place," said the disciples. "You give them something to eat," Jesus replies, and the disciples, who earlier boasted about their success, are faced with their inadequacy. The story of the feeding of the five thousand (Luke 9:10–17) again reveals Jesus' flexibility and willingness to jettison his own agenda in order to respond to the needs of others. Constantly his life weaves in and out of the longings of people he meets until together they are able to dance the joy of God. Yet I never see Jesus as an exhausted caregiver or as an activist wrung dry from unceasing work among the needy. I suspect that it was his practice of regular time apart with God that sustained him in ministry. Mark tells us that Jesus set aside time in the predawn hours for prayer and then responded willingly to the disciples who came to tell him that the crowd was looking for him. But Jesus did not return to the place of his successful proclamation of God's grace; instead he responds: "Let us go on to the neighboring towns, so that I may

proclaim the message there also; for that is what I came out to do"
(Mark 1:38). Jesus was not driven by ego needs; he cultivated an
open, flexible spirit that took time to listen to God.

REFLECTING WITH SCRIPTURE
Mark 9:2–8

How is flexibility manifested as you continue your faith journey?
Are there fears that you try to avoid that present themselves as
opportunities to engage in creative movement and beauty?

PRAYER

God of mobility, your beauty is manifested throughout creation.
Help us to stay open to your marvelous shaping of all creatures and
to appreciate those that cause us difficulty. May we listen for your
Word spoken in our intentional times of prayer, but also in everyday
activities that sometimes keep us too busy. Show us where we need
to let go of rigid patterns that are no longer life-giving so that our
hours may flow with the Spirit of grace, interweaving beauty, and
purpose, as we move ever deeper into life. Amen.

TRUST

Gee-up

When I was three-years-old and went to Sunday School for the first time, I distinguished myself by singing a song for the group, unaware that it was not a Christian hymn or chorus:

Gee up Neddy to the fair
What shall we buy when we get there?
A ha'penny bun and a penny pear
Gee up Neddy to the fair.

At that tender age, I had not learned to distinguish between sacred and secular; perhaps it was a pity that all too soon I began to compartmentalize what did and did not belong to God. There was some amusement on the part of the teacher, but she accepted my offering and the innocence with which I sang. At home I had a "hobby-horse" I loved, so the song seemed especially to express my delight in childhood play. I can still hear the echo of my mother's voice urging me along with "Gee up" when I was being too slow as we walked to the park or the store. It was many years before I met a real horse, but these beautiful animals were alive in my imagination and play.

In the biblical narratives, horses are sometimes portrayed as

stubborn, difficult creatures: "Do not be like a horse or a mule without understanding, whose temper must be curbed with bit and bridle" (Psalm 32:9); "A whip for the horse, a bridle for the donkey, and a rod for the back of fools" (Proverbs 26:3). With one exception, the horses I have encountered have learned to trust the humans who raised and rode them and have responded well to firm but kind training. The exception was a very large and powerful animal assigned to me a few years ago when I went with a group on a beach horse-riding excursion. First, with my arthritic bones, I had difficulty getting onto the horse, and he must have sensed I was an amateur and very unsure of myself as well as him. We set off on a wet afternoon through woods near the beach, where dripping Spanish moss wrapped itself around my head and the horse stumbled through deep puddles. He had a mind of his own and attempts to rein him in were useless. I did not trust him, and clearly, he did not trust my riding ability or authority. The experience was unlike any other, including the first horse I learned to feed from my open hand. My mother had tucked some carrots in her bag when we left the house, and we went to stand by a fence at the edge of a nearby field where horses grazed. Soon they approached us, but to a small child they seemed very large and frightening, so I drew back. I wanted very much to offer food, but I was afraid I would be bitten. Mother helped me to uncurl my tight fingers, allowing the carrot to rest in my upturned palm and slowly to move within reach of the horse's mouth. Soft, warm lips embraced the carrot as the great creature gently took it from my hand.

There are so many wonderful stories in literature about wild creatures who have learned to trust the humans they encountered. The fox in the story of *The Little Prince* taught the hero that he must wait patiently for many days. In his own time, the fox slowly came closer as he learned to trust the child. Sometimes, like the fox, we need a lot of time when it comes to trusting God. No matter how many times in the past we have been gently received and nurtured, there remains within us a tentativeness as we approach the Holy One. Can I really trust God with my life? Or perhaps more to the point, can God trust me? Maybe I have come close in the past and then scurried away into the bushes because I am afraid I may be hurt. There is a mutuality about real trust, and it grows over a lifetime of dealing with hurt, disappointment, and running away, as well as through times of deep communion.

Among the many biblical verses I memorized when I was in Sunday School—all of them then in the language of the King James Version of the Bible—one continues to challenge me today: "Trust in the LORD with all thine heart; and lean not unto thine own understanding. In all thy ways acknowledge him, and he shall direct thy paths" (Proverbs 3:5–6, KJV). What would that kind of trust look like? If I hold out my hand toward the Creator, will God not gently take what I offer, my little trust, and help me gradually to come closer? And in time I may trust enough to climb onto the divine back and allow God to find the path I thought was unsafe or obscure. Perhaps the horse I thought was determined to scare me and go its own way was actually much more sure of the path than I was and needed me to loosen the reins. Perhaps he was trying to say "Trust me! I have carried many inexperienced riders like yourself, and I know the way through these woods and will bring you safely onto the shore." Perhaps God invites me to let go instead of hanging on to the way I think is best. Who knows what new paths may open up and what kind of beauty awaits me round the next turn?

REFLECTING WITH SCRIPTURE
Isaiah 12:2–6
How are you invited to deepen your trust in God at this time? Do you recall moments of confusion or fear when you relinquished your own control and begun to discern new paths?

PRAYER
Divine Teacher, help me to trust that you will lead me along good paths, though I may not see the way ahead. Amen.

TRUTH

Caws They Can

Often I sit in the mornings watching the birds. Carolina chicadees, golden finches, blue jays, cardinals, sparrows, downy woodpeckers, and many more come to feast in my yard and bathe in the birdbath conveniently placed near their feeders. Then there are the crows. A single harsh squawk is followed by a cacophony of screeching, and the dark, raggedy birds begin to gather in the trees. There they perch like menacing black-suited clerics, who scream at the unwary and pronounce hellfire on unrepentant sinners. There is nothing obviously subtle about crows: They are raucous, unpretentious, and full of themselves. Crows do not spread bejeweled tail feathers like the peacock or flaunt multicolored wings like the parrot, but seem comfortable with their plain, blue-black dress. Sharp, beady eyes serve them well, for they can spot roadkill or flung birdseed from afar and quickly announce their finds to one another. They wait in the branches, now silent, until the boldest crow lands on the ground, grabs a piece of bread in its beak, and flies a few feet off to consume breakfast in safety. One by one the others follow while the cats look on, longing to provide a little crowd control in the yard.

In my imagination, crows represent truth-tellers and remind me of the prophets in Hebrew Scripture, or John the Baptist, who stands in the line of proclaimers of God's call to righteousness and

truth. They do not mince words or try to tone down the message, for they are passionate about justice and impatient with any kind of religious posturing. Unlike some of us in the Christian tradition who would prefer to ignore the imprecatory psalms and prophetic tirades that call for vengeance, they make it plain that such feelings of revenge are real in our hearts even when we are afraid to own them with our lips. Prophets, and crows, are not pretenders; theirs are "in your face" unrelenting voices that are difficult to ignore. They are a gift to us, especially when we are tempted to bask in our niceness. The crow is honored among indigenous people of the United States, but is seen as sinister by others who have not learned to appreciate its many gifts, including highway cleanup. I wish to honor the crow, whose gift to me is a challenge to deeper integrity, including a willingness to own my desire for vindication and revenge.

Some years ago an experience of betrayal left me raw, vengeful, and caught in self-pitying hatred of the perpetrator. I tried to pray, but as soon as I brought the situation into consciousness, I was off into a fantasy world of revenge. I wanted to see him suffer, to see his reputation hit the dust, so that the world could see this highly respected man for an insensitive fraud. Of course I knew the teaching of Jesus that we should forgive not once but seventy times seven. I also knew that the inner rage was hurting only me and that I would not know peace until I was willing to let go of anger. But I couldn't do it. Day after day I prayed for the grace to forgive and move on, but the hurt continued to fester like a wound from which the scab was repeatedly torn off. I tried to pray for the betrayer, but quickly plunged again into resentment. Slowly I began to realize that some injuries take a long time to heal and need to be tended with love and compassion. Instead of demanding instant justification and increasing my discomfort by rehearsing scenarios again and again, I needed to love my wounded self, to honestly express to God my desire for revenge, and to live with an awareness of my inability to lovingly forgive. I needed to give myself time to heal. My prayer became a commitment not to pretend a Christian maturity I did not possess, but to go on living with the pain until I could honestly forgive and let go.

Many weeks later I was reading the story of the sick man at the pool of Beth-zatha near the Sheep Gate in Jerusalem. It was a place of hopelessness and resentment where people with many diseases gathered in hope of being the first to step into the pool after the waters bubbled up each day. Those who were blind, lame, and paralyzed huddled within the five porticoes waiting, often without hope, for the chance to be well. One man had waited for thirty-eight years in this spot, but day after day someone else always made it into the pool ahead of him since he could not move without help. When Jesus enters this place of sickness, he notices and speaks to the man: "Do you want to be made well?" he asks (John 5:6). On the surface, the question seems to be insensitive and ludicrous; of course the man wanted to be healed, why else would he be here? But there are compensations for illness—no doubt the man had become accustomed to his paralysis after so many years of dependence on the charity of others. He had become accustomed to his sense of helplessness and hopelessness, and healing would require a radical change in lifestyle and attitude. Did he really want to be healed? It is clear from his reply that he no longer entertained the idea of change, for he began to recite the impossibility of ever getting into the pool. Jesus says to him: "'Stand up, take your mat and walk' At once the man was made well, and he took up his mat and began to walk" (John 5:8–9). Jesus had a way of identifying the *kairos*, the strategic moment for action, and his imperious command resulted in healing before the man even understood what he was doing. The paralyzed one walked.

As I read this story, putting myself in the place of the sick man, I heard Jesus ask, "Do you want to be healed of your resentment and anger?" And in all honesty I had to reply, "No. I want to get even," but added, "but I am willing to wait for the grace to forgive and let go." This became my prayer until one day I heard the question and was ready to say "Yes." It was a moment of liberation and joy. I would like to say that I have never slipped back into the memory and pain of the betrayal, but that would not be crow-honesty. The person in question continues to be deeply admired by many, and when someone tells me enthusiastically they have listened to one of his addresses, there is a bubbling up of envy and resentment. I want to tell them the "truth"—*my* truth—about this man and point out his failure. But now I quickly become aware of this response, and each time repeat my "yes" to Jesus' question, "Do you want to be healed?" and I can even love the lapsed, resentful me who is tempted to wallow in self-righteousness. I can also laugh a bit at the silliness of choosing to pick away at the past wound as I return to the God of healing grace and compassion.

REFLECTING WITH SCRIPTURE
Psalm 55
How do you respond to the psalmist's experience and expression of feelings?

PRAYER

Physician of our souls, set us free from old wounds that keep us locked in hopeless prisons of self-righteous anger. Help us to forgive as you forgive us, to love as you love us, to hope as you have taught us to hope in the resurrection life of Christ. Give us grace to know ourselves as loveable and fallible disciples whose prayer is sometimes a squawk of vengeance. Give us the assurance that you alone are able to receive safely and respond lovingly to our deepest desires, even those of which we are ashamed. Amen.

WISDOM

Comings and Goings

Like most people, I do not enjoy preparing my tax return, and since I now live in the United States, April 15 marks that nail-biting deadline. But there is another event I anticipate with great joy on or around "tax day": The wood thrush returns to my yard with her clear fluted song. She has arrived as early as the 13th of April and one year kept me waiting anxiously until 21st, but always she has come, and for four months her voice awakens the dawn. A few *po po po* notes are followed by a climbing gurgle that ends with a trilled whistle, and after this is repeated a few times, other bird calls begin to join the early morning chorus. Even on the dullest summer morning, the wood thrush provides my wake-up call. How does she know when to come and when it is time to migrate to Florida or the warmer southwestern states? The wood thrush lives by an inner wisdom that is beyond my knowing; she is attuned to the rhythms of creation that pulsate within her tiny body. I envy her.

Our western "pre-packaged" lifestyle has a way of distancing us from the ancient wisdom our ancestors knew as they lived more deeply in sync with nature and the seasons. Farmers knew when to plant, not by a calendar date, but by close observation of weather patterns, the movement of animals, and an innate sense of time. Cooperation with creation characterized their work, rather than a

determination to dominate and control. They knew the delight of the first-ripened corn, fresh strawberries, or new-dug potatoes, none of which were obtainable year-round from importers or freezers. Of course, they also knew the deep disappointment and loss caused by an out-of-season storm or insect invasion—but such occurrences gave reason for celebration in the years of abundant harvest. The wood thrush is a gracious reminder that there is more to life than schedules, deadlines, and attempts to manipulate the world to meet our demands. There is a deeper pulse at the very heart of life that will bless us and reveal the wisdom of the Creator if we will but pause to listen.

I write this reflection on July 30, 2005. I rose at 3:30 a.m. in order to be at the airport for a very early commuter plane that would connect me with a long international flight to Johannesburg. Yesterday I checked flight details and learned that despite a recent

airline strike, all was now well and I should not expect problems. At the check-in desk today, the clerk told me that my overseas flight was cancelled, and there were no available seats until August 2 through this or any other connection. I was stunned as I stood with packed bags ready to be on my way, after days of planning six weeks of care for my house, yard, and cats. This was not supposed to happen. There must be an alternative, a way to satisfy MY agenda, MY schedule—the world is supposed to revolve around MY needs. But it was not to be. After hauling bags back in the house and greeting the cats, I went out onto the screen porch where I could hear water pouring over rocks. I tried to be still. A honking flock of geese passed overhead and sunlight caught the tips of a Norfolk pine, turning them emerald green. I sat for a few minutes listening, seeing, smelling the late summer day, and began to relinquish the demand for control. Here the rhythm of the earth, the wisdom of creation beckoned and I found, at least for a while, that I was at home on earth instead of trying to twist its rhythms into a shape that suited my agenda. I was helped further when I opened a book of poetry by Mary Oliver, *Why I Wake Early*,[3] and read in her poem "The Wren from Carolina," "all things are inventions of holiness."
I was once again drawn into an awareness of what it really means to be human in a world full of wonder. And at that moment, the wood thrush sang, perhaps for the last time this season.

Luke 19:41–44 tells us of the profound sadness of Jesus as he looked out over the city of Jerusalem. Jesus saw a city in danger of destruction and a people who had no vision for peace-making, no true understanding of its vocation as a beacon of hope in the world. Leaders were more interested in commerce than worship, and they were using the most sacred place, the temple, as a market place. Inhumanity, greed, and exploitation of the innocent had become the structure through which many religious leaders were exercising power, and they had lost touch with God's rhythm of compassion for people and planet. Jesus weeps at the sight of it all and says: "You did not recognize the time of your visitation from God" (Luke

---

3. Mary Oliver, *Why I Wake Early* (Boston: Beacon Press, 2004).

19:44). God had visited them day by day, sometimes through prophets, but also through the "signs of the times" and the creatures whose land they shared. In another place Jesus says: "Look at the birds of the air; they neither sow nor reap nor gather into barns yet your heavenly Father feeds them" (Matthew 6:26). The birds are teachers too, and they seem to live with more sense than a lot of humans because they do not become consumed with stockpiling "stuff" for the future. Jesus taught his followers to look at the world of nature and learn from it. Plants, sheep, weather patterns, trees, flowers, wheat, foxes, birds, camels—all have the capacity to teach us how to live if we will but pay attention to their presence.

Jesus did not live with cyberspace, airline and space travel, scientific research with its inevitable ethical questions, or even with telephone or postal service, but the gospels suggest he was as busy as most of us are today. The difference seems to be that he was aware of how easy it was to be mindlessly caught up in the demands that were made upon him, and he took steps to remain vigilant to each moment. Sometimes he withdrew even from the disciples so that he could breathe more deeply into the rhythm of grace and know how to live the moment. A sense of time as *kairos* (the right moment or fullness of time) rather than *chronos* (clock time) determined how Jesus responded to life and responsibilities. In a pressing crowd of people as he responded to a request to go with a synagogue official whose little daughter was sick, he was sensitive to a single touch from a distressed hemorrhaging woman (Mark 5:21–34), and he stopped to acknowledge and touch her. He was attuned to her need and not consumed with a sense of importance or hurry. Jesus listened to the rhythm of human life, of Creator and creation in the interconnected web of the universe. He listened to God's heartbeat and lived, like the wood thrush, in the "now" of grace.

REFLECTING WITH SCRIPTURE
Proverbs 8:1–11
Do you spend time simply "being" in nature? Have you discovered wisdom in creation and creatures to enable to live in the present moment?

PRAYER

Sophia, God of all Wisdom, you walk in our midst with gifts to offer, but we turn away from you, too busy with our daily tasks to notice your presence. Jesus embodied your grace, but people turned away from him too, preferring choices that impoverished their lives. Help us to take time to listen to the rhythms of nature and our animal friends who live simply so that we may clear away the clutter of busyness. Help us to grow in mindfulness and to receive each moment as an opportunity for hope. Amen.

LAUGHTER

Monkey Business

After a twenty-hour flight from Atlanta to Johannesburg, I was more than happy to see my friend waiting to greet me in the crowded airport. A strike had delayed my arrival by three days, and it was a relief to settle into Annie's small car as we made our way to the Pilanesberg Game Reserve. We checked into the Bakubung Lodge and pulled open the sliding French doors to allow the fresh, warm air to circulate. Bakubung means place of the hippo, and we were to see many hippos over the next couple of days. But first we both needed a nap. We stretched out on the twin beds and both of us had drifted into sleep when a loud rustling startled us. I thought that Annie must be unwrapping one of the snack packages she had brought, and I later learned that she was thinking *I* was the noise maker. A moment later we discovered the real culprit: A monkey had come into the room and was helping herself to the packet of cookies the hotel provided along with tea-making equipment. From that time on, the monkey was a constant presence just outside the room, entertaining us by chasing off competitors, and waiting for another unguarded moment when she might again help herself to our snacks.

Monkeys, and their larger cousins baboons, are endlessly funny and sometimes destructive. They love to jump on cars—and often

into them—looking for a handout. They will tear out windshield wipers, antennas, or any other removable objects while passengers watch helplessly. Because they frequently carry rabies, it is wise to heed the many warnings to refrain from feeding or coming too close to these entertaining creatures.

Shortly after the encounter in Pilanesberg, I went to Cape Town and my hosts offered to drive me to Cape Point, the rugged place where the Indian and Atlantic oceans meet. We parked and prepared to walk up the well-defined path rather than take the funicular to the top. Along the way, we watched a mother baboon with her baby and saw several more of the animals leaping over rocks. The climb was fairly steep, and we stopped to rest at an overlook, where we were able to look down several hundred feet to waves crashing on the rocks below. I was absorbed by the beauty of the place until a sharp intake of breath caused me to turn around. A very large male baboon was tugging at the handles of the Harrod's tote that my hostess was holding. "Let him have it!" her husband said as the baboon bared his ugly yellow teeth. The baboon quickly snatched the tote and moved a few feet away where he sat on a rock and, one by one, picked out and discarded the contents of the bag. A silk scarf floated to the ground, binoculars crashed on to the rocky path, and other items followed until the baboon found a small container of mini mints. He cracked the brittle plastic with his teeth, emptied the contents into his mouth, tossed down the tote, and stomped away, apparently disgusted that there was no greater reward for his effort. After a stunned silence, we gathered up the contents of the tote, laughing at the audacity of the baboon as we continued up the path.

Almost at the top, we once again stopped for a few moments, and while we were scanning the ocean for whales, the baboon crept up once again. This time, he grabbed the lovely Gucci purse my hostess carried, and he became more aggressive as she resisted his attempts to carry it off. Once again, all she could do was let go and watch as the baboon took off with the bag containing her cell phone, billfold, and many other valuable items. Sensing that the monitors who were responsible for visitor safety were approaching, the baboon did not unpack the purse nearby, but ran around rocks to where there was a steep drop into the ocean. He did not let go, as we feared he might, but found a comfortable point by a rocky outcrop, where he efficiently unzipped each compartment and again tossed the contents to the ground. Fortunately, the two monitors who appeared were experienced at negotiating the hazardous promontory, and they were able to climb down and retrieve the Gucci bag and its contents. At first, my hostess thought that nothing was missing, but then remembered that she had carried a container of prescription tranquilizers. The pills looked remarkably like mini mints. We never did see the baboon again, but suspected he had passed out, happily drugged with a beatific smile on his face, no longer a threat to unwary visitors. It was amusing to note that he seemed unattracted to my rather plain, canvas, healthyback bag. This was a baboon with fine tastes.

Many animals bring a smile to our faces as we watch their playful antics. Some seem funny to us simply by their appearance and suggest that the Creator has a sense of humor. The camel with its hump, long-necked giraffes, leaping kangaroos, ducks that waddle on land, and many more creatures delight us with their presence. And we need to laugh! There is so much happening in our world that tempts us to lose hope in God, and we find ourselves feeling powerless, dejected, and fearful. Without denying the reality of so much suffering and need, we owe it to ourselves to find occasions for humor and healthy laughter. Although the Gospel writers do not speak of Jesus laughing, he uses images that cause us to smile: amusing examples include a camel trying to pass through a needle's eye and someone attempting to remove a tiny speck from a neighbor's eye while a large plank protrudes from his or her own. The Hebrew Scriptures contain stories and vignettes that make us smile at human foolishness and invite us to find ourselves in the characters portrayed. The short book of Jonah offers one such portrait.

Jonah is a man of God who knows what he is to do and where he is to go, but heads off in the wrong direction. God longs to include all people in the circle of belonging, but Jonah wants to pick and choose the in-crowd, and that definitely does not include the people of Nineveh. The trouble is, God is just too merciful for Jonah, who wants nothing to do with his assignment. We know well the story of the storm, during which Jonah is tossed overboard only to be swallowed by a big fish. Inside its belly, Jonah composes a psalm that contains a graphic description of his weedy sojourn at the bottom of the ocean and his promise to do what he has vowed to God. The fish, having carried Jonah to where God wanted him to go in the first place, spits the reluctant prophet up onto the beach. The picture of Jonah, stinking of fish and dazed —and of a relieved fish glad to be rid of a severe bout of indigestion —is amusing, to say the least. Jonah goes to preach in the great city of Nineveh, and there is a mass repentance and God does not punish the inhabitants for their wickedness after all. But this is not the end of the story. The last scene finds Jonah outside the city, sitting inside a booth he has made and pouting like a three-year-old or a teenager who has been given a curfew. Jonah grumbles at God, upbraids the Creator who is altogether too merciful, and says he would rather die than live with the way things are.

Scholars suggest that this little story was written after the Babylonian exile to challenge those religious leaders whose zeal for reform led to an exclusionary policy against others who did not keep the Law as they understood it. It is also a timeless tale that compels readers to remember that God has no outcasts and that running away from vocation is fruitless. At the same time, we are invited to smile at ourselves, at our sometimes immature behavior. We are reminded through the story—and through the antics of creatures like the baboon—that God is right there smiling us back into obedience.

REFLECTING WITH SCRIPTURE
Matthew 11:28–30
Do you recall times when animal antics have called you to delight and laughter? Have you ever caught yourself behaving like a rebellious child because God seems to be asking you to go places or do things that are unattractive to you?

PRAYER
Christ of the easy yoke, help me walk beside you. Sometimes I feel overburdened with responsibility, and it seems like you are asking me to open my heart to those who are outside my circle. Please show me myself when I resent your grace toward others; help me to smile at my rebellious acting out and to turn back to you so that we may travel a straight path together. Amen.

CREATIVITY

Wonder Webs

For several days Diana, an elderly neighbor, watched a spider creating her web between two gateposts. A long gossamer thread spanned the gap above the gate and the intricately woven web hung shivering below. Each morning the web was dew-covered, a thing of beauty that sparkled like diamonds in the early light, and Diana delighted in its radiance. She felt such deep respect for the spider's labor that she took the long way round her house into the rose garden instead of using the more convenient gate. The spider became an honored companion who taught many lessons by simply being her spider-self.

Then hurricane Hugo made landfall in Charleston, South Carolina. He destroyed many coastland dwellings before continuing his devastating march inland. He snatched and destroyed trailer homes, felled pine trees, tore down power lines, and left a trail of destruction in his path. Taking refuge in her basement, Diana wondered if anything would be spared in her beautifully landscaped yard. When the storm finally blew itself out, she ventured outside. Shingles were torn from the roof and debris covered her property, but she suffered no major loss. Diana looked sadly at the battered gate and then at the place where the web had hung. To her amazement and delight, it remained, undamaged between the gateposts.

The supple strength and delicate design of the web proved stronger than the deluge and storm. The spider and her creation were intact.

The Creator makes things that will last. Standing beneath the great redwoods of California or looking out over the ancient Appalachian Mountains, I am awed by the durability of God's handiwork. Despite devastating assaults on this fragile planet, many of them the result of human abuse and exploitation, the resilient earth holds fast. "God don't make no junk," proclaims a Southern preacher, echoing the refrain of the Creator in Genesis 1: "Behold, it is very good." Diana observed the spider, a tiny creator of webs, and saw beyond the strength of her woven threads an image of the creative energy that flows through our genes also. "Am I weaving my life with strong threads of trust in the Creator of all things?" she asked as she spent time in silent reflection later that day. The first question led to others. How do we fulfill our vocation to create a sustainable life for all people? When we are assaulted by storms of fear that drain us emotionally, will we hold fast to the Anchor of our souls, Christ, who strengthens us to withstand each onslaught of doubt?

The psalmist writes: "It was you [God] who formed my inward parts; you knit me together in my mother's womb" (Psalm 139:13). The Creator is the architect of our wonderfully woven lives, but as we grow, we choose how to work with the threads of grace. We weave strength and durability into our inner being through prayerful disciplines that help us pay attention to the divine Weaver. Commitment to a daily time with God is the central thread that holds the structure together. Reflection on the continuing story of God's people, and our own place in the community of faith, keeps hope alive. Sometimes the web is damaged by pain, loss, disappointment, or fear, but as we tend the broken threads, the Creator helps us to repair what has been hurt. The hurricane Hugos of the soul cannot dislodge the strong threads of trust that are woven out of a lifetime of faithful discipleship.

Creativity is essential for healthy human life. As a teenager, I developed a passion for oil painting and became quite accomplished at the art. I loved the flexibility of oil paint, and I was able to "lose" myself in imagination as the painting took shape. One day I was so absorbed by what I was doing that I tossed an oily rag into the fireplace where it burst into flames and set the chimney on fire. As time went on, I painted less and less. I became an ardent member of a fundamentalist church, where we were rewarded for "head knowledge" of the Bible, and I entered a time of depression. Little did I realize that I had become sick, in part, because I had let go of my creativity. Over the years, I have learned that I need to create, not necessarily with brush and palette, but through making my home beautiful within and without, writing poetry, singing, and occasionally working with clay. Creativity is not about "coloring between the lines," but finding the place where imagination is engaged. From stargazing to animal husbandry, knitting to cabinet making, fly fishing to shape-note singing, gardening to writing a novel—all these activities and countless more are invitations for us to live our way into the image of the Creator lodged deep within us. When prayer becomes dull and desire for spiritual growth wanes, it may be a reminder that there are many ways to participate with God on our life journey, and engaging creativity is one of the most important.

The twelfth-century mystic Hilegard of Bingen was a remarkable woman who is remembered as a musician, theologian, healer, and prophet, and the dynamic abbess of a Benedictine monastery on the Rhine. Early in her life she learned that some of her visionary experiences posed problems for those whose imaginations were limited and understanding of theology strictly delineated. For this reason, she kept quiet about her "illuminations" and went through a period of serious illness. It was after her spiritual adviser told her that she must express the content of her visions that Hildegard began to recover her health. At her adviser's instruction, the astonishing illuminations Hildegard had received were painted to portray images of God that are intimate, inclusive, and filled with compassion for humanity and the "web of the universe." Sometimes what is imprisoned within us may make us sick. We need to give expression to the glorious power of imagination and creativity that reflects the divine. We may not be Beethoven or Michelangelo, but we can at least be like the tiny spider who blessed Diana through the dark and difficult days of a storm.

REFLECTING WITH SCRIPTURE
Colossians 1:15–20
How do you tend the web of your soul? Do you notice any places that are weakened through the battering of life's storms?

PRAYER
Holy Weaver, you created our inmost being before we uttered our first cries on the earth, and you have taught us how to grow in trust and faithful service through the example of Jesus. By the power of the Holy Spirit, keep us strong in faith, vigilant through stormy times, and ready to mend the broken places of our lives. We pray that our lives may sparkle with your radiance so that others may see the beauty of your gentle strength in us. May the strong threads of grace become visible in our words and actions. Amen.

ATTENTIVENESS

Paws for Prayer

A sharp-eyed Dominican sister was returning to her retreat house one evening when she noticed a stirring in the bushes beside the highway. She stopped and waited. A tiny gray kitten, motherless, hungry, and very frightened, crouched among the leaves but skittered away when Sister Trina tried to rescue her. It took a long time, but after patient and persistent efforts, the kitten was lifted to safety. The kitten spent the night in a guest room, where she was given food, water, and a soft bed. The retreat house was home to a large animal population. Native animals —deer, fox, rabbit, opossum, raccoon— roamed the woods and numerous stray dogs and cats lived with the sisters. They did not need one more mouth to feed. On the following morning, Sister Trina took the kitten to a local vet, who guessed that she was barely seven weeks old. He treated her for worms and the vast number of fleas that had taken up residence in her fur.

Meanwhile, I was living at Holy Savior Priory, a small monastic house of the Anglican Benedictine Order of the Holy Cross, about twenty-five miles from the Dominican Retreat House. I had been at the monastery as program director for six months when I decided it was time to visit the sisters. I went with one of the monks, and after touring the retreat house, we heard the story of the rescued kitten. I wanted a cat to share my small cabin, and the sisters had prayed for

someone to adopt her. The kitten came home with me, and since it was the feast day of St. Boniface in the Liturgical calendar, I gave her the name Bonnie. Bonnie was my faithful companion and teacher for almost eighteen years.

The Rule of St. Benedict begins with the words "Listen my child . . . with the ear of your heart," and the structure of the monastic day supports attentive listening to God. Each day begins and ends in silence; the psalms are chanted and Scripture read at the offices (services of worship), and Eucharist is celebrated daily. Time is set aside for personal prayer, work, reading, and rest, and the community gathers for meals and recreation. Monastic life is focused on paying attention to holy Presence through reflection on the Bible, respectful interaction with others, including the care of guests, and labor undertaken prayerfully. It was a blessing to join the monks in this balanced daily rhythm, but during the five years I lived with the community, I also received great wisdom from Bonnie. She always seemed to live in the moment; she knew when to be still and when to play and went about her cat life with focused attention.

When Bonnie was almost ready to come into heat, I took her back to the vet to be spayed. The following day I picked her up, and clearly, she was feeling a lot of discomfort. It was hard for me to see her pain, knowing that I had subjected her to the surgery, so I did all I could to distract her. I stroked her head, set her favorite food before her, made her a special soft bed. But nothing seemed to work. Bonnie chose a sunny spot on the carpet, where she curled up with her pain, ignoring my attempts to make her more comfortable. The next day she went outside and was soon prowling along a tree branch to where a bird taunted her. In a culture that tries to minimize and mask physical and psychological pain with a pill or therapy, Bonnie showed me another way—the way of paying attention. I am not suggesting that we suffer unnecessarily or reject modern medicine, but that sometimes we are in pain because we do not live mindfully. My own inclination is to do too much, to be so driven by work that finally my body rebels and I succumb to sickness. Then I act as if the world will stop turning because I cannot keep all the appointments in my calendar. While Bonnie was recovering, there was a jingle on TV promoting a drug company whose product promised instant relief: "I haven't got time for the pain." Benedictine wisdom invites us to be present to the difficult and painful experiences of our lives as much as to the joyful celebrations—and through all to grow toward wholeness.

Bonnie and I moved to North Carolina in 1991, and she continued to teach me and bless others by her attitude of presence to each moment. Sometimes she sat in the window, body quivering, watching intently as squirrels played in the yard. I often longed to pray like that, undistracted, tingling with excitement at the playful presence of the Creator. Sometimes Bonnie would sense sadness in me or in one of the people who came for spiritual guidance and she would respond with her gentle presence. Bonnie was a shy cat who did not readily approach strangers, but I watched her come into the room when someone was in grief, walk towards them and jump onto the chair. She then waited for consent before stepping into the stranger's lap and curling up. The grieving person would begin to rhythmically stroke Bonnie's soft fur as I sat, silently present to the tears that flowed and the painful memories that were being released. The Jesuit writer Jeanne Pierre De Caussade coined the phrase "the sacrament of the present moment" and described all our daily tasks and experiences as shadows which hide the divine.[4] It is through loving attention to all our activities that the shadows pass and we see God at the heart of life. And often an animal will teach us far more about being present than any number of text books or models for meditation.

REFLECTING WITH SCRIPTURE
Luke 2:25–38
What helps you to notice the holy in the ordinary? Try paying attention to your inner life by keeping a journal and reflecting each day on rhythms that are life-giving and God-centered.

PRAYER
Listening God, give us open ears and hearts as we ponder the wisdom in all your creatures. Help us pay attention to our work and experiences and to penetrate the shadows that hide you. When grief or loss come our way, may we be blessed by the gentle presence of creatures who teach us to find your healing grace as we give time to the pain. Amen.

---

4. Jean-Pierre de Caussade, *Self-Abandonment to Divine Providence* (London: Burns and Oates, 1933), 32–33. The book is now available under the more inviting title *The Sacrament of the Present Moment* (San Francisco: HarperSanFrancisco).

GRACE

Psalms of the Salt Marsh

One bright Summer Saturday, a diverse group of parishioners and friends made their way from New York City to Freeport, Long Island. We gathered in a meadow close to the water's edge and sat around picnic tables as our poet-naturalist, Max, instructed us on observing the natural world. "We are going to write psalms," he told us, and quickly reassured the fearful among us that we would simply be using existing psalms but writing our own observation into the structure. We picked up our notebooks and pens and followed Max, who taught us to open our eyes and ears to the world around us. It took a little time to tune in to the sound of cicadas and to the gentle lapping of the water and the sound of the leaves rustling in a gentle breeze. Our eyes moved from seeing only a meadow to observing the tiny creatures who inhabited the salt marsh. On the shore we saw many birds and, in the far distance, the twin towers of the World Trade Center, reminding us of the proximity of the city. Standing motionless in the shallow water, a blue heron observed our approach. She was a beautiful creature, graceful, poised, and we waited silently as she plunged her long beak into the bay for mummichog. The heron was a special gift to city dwellers accustomed to seeing few birds except the scavenging pigeons who left their mark on parked cars, sidewalks, and, sometimes, the heads of unwary walkers.

The psalms we shared later in the day expressed our joy in
spending a few hours away from the buildings and traffic sounds of
the city. Each psalm was different and the observations of nature
varied, but almost all focused on the wonder of seeing the blue heron
so close to Manhattan. I think often of that day, especially when
I walk around our local lake in the early dawn, where sometimes a

lone blue heron waits near the shore. She is always a special gift, a grace that blesses my day and draws me into a prayer of desire to wait in God's stillness and to remember in the midst of busyness that each moment is gift. Sometimes the heron balances gracefully on one of her pencil-thin legs, poised like a ballerina, and stretching her long neck. And so I pause, watch her for a while, and give thanks for her blue-gray beauty reflected in the shallow water at the lake's edge. Some of the early morning joggers run past, unaware of the silent bird who graces the day.

God's grace is abundant, and one of the most beautiful images in Scripture pictures God as a beautiful woman, Wisdom (Sophia), who comes into the city with many gifts for the people who have gathered. Wisdom calls out, "Take my instruction instead of silver, and knowledge rather than choice gold; for wisdom is better than jewels" (Proverbs 8:10–11), and she goes on to declare that she was present at the creation of the world (8:22f). In the Wisdom of Solomon, we learn even more about the qualities of Wisdom: "Wisdom is radiant and unfading, and she is easily discerned by those who love her, and is found by those who seek her. She hastens to make herself known to those who desire her. One who rises early to seek her will have no difficulty, for she will be found sitting at the gate" (6:12–14). In the era between the gathering of Hebrew Scriptures and the Christian writings, it appears that there was a blending of the concept of God as the Word (masculine) and Wisdom (feminine), and the author of the Fourth Gospel probably had this thought in mind when he composed his prologue. John says that Jesus is the Word, who from the very beginning was with God, was God, and through him all things were made. Jesus, like the figure of Wisdom, comes to his own people offering them the price-less gift of eternal life, but not all are ready to receive the gift. Some turn away, preferring to remain in darkness instead of allowing themselves to be illuminated by the Christ-light. Those who receive him are incorporated into the family of God through a new birth; they receive eternal life as a present reality, life in all its fullness (John 10:10).

The Long Island heron was grace-full; so were each of the people who gathered that day and allowed their gifts of creativity to be expressed. Marshland and meadow, bugs and birds, wind and water all spoke to us of the grace of God and invited us to claim the blessings of our humanity. One older member of our group was frail, living with a lot of pain, but she celebrated the gift of time away from her apartment and the presence of her toddler grandson. An out-of-work actor who spent her days trying to find employment and wondering if her decision to move to New York City was a mistake, discovered fresh hope and energy through the day of respite. A couple of teenagers who were doubtful about joining a group of adults on an outing to Long Island, each wrote outstanding psalms and became fascinated by the creatures of the marsh. And a woman who was CEO of a very successful executive search company found that the day she thought she could not spare away from her busy office proved to be exactly the kind of "retreat" she needed in order to rest mind, body, and spirit. It required commitment to take a full day away from the city, but as we gifted ourselves with recreative time, we received gifts in abundance.

At the close of the day, we gathered around a picnic table where earlier we had shared lunch. Now we gathered to share bread and wine in a simple service of Holy Communion. The homily was preached by the whole community, as each person shared the experiences of the day and gave thanks for gifts received. The heron was frequently mentioned and much gratitude was expressed to Max who had opened our eyes to the grace-filled world around us and within us. We returned to the city refreshed and ready to allow gratitude to grow by our attentive presence to the abundant gifts of God's love in daily life.

REFLECTING WITH SCRIPTURE
James 1:17–18
When have you given yourself a gift of time to simply be in creation? How do you express your own creative gifts and share them with others?

PRAYER
Creator of beauty and grace, open our eyes to your presence in the everydayness of our lives as well as in those times apart when we rest

in the beauty of creation. Help us to greet each new day with open hands and hearts, ready to receive from your Son, who is both Word and Wisdom, the gifts we need to live thankfully. Through us, may your grace be revealed to all people so that they may hear the invitation to live as members of your family and live life in all its fullness now and always. Amen.

LOSS

Seeing Red

As my little blue Mazda made its way up the mile-long dirt road to the Priory, Little Red left the corner of the field where he was grazing and lumbered toward the fence. "Little" hardly described him. He had received the name when he was born to his father Red, a very handsome breeding bull with a large progeny. Now Little Red was a huge animal, and we had developed a routine acquaintance. When he saw the car, Little Red would approach the fence, and I then spent several minutes scratching and massaging his enormous head. I had grown up being terrified of bulls, and they had frequently inhabited my nightmares as a child. Once on a walk in a country lane with my aunt, a large bovine rounded the corner, and in alarm we ran to hide behind some bushes. My aunt was convinced it was the bull that belonged to a neighboring farmer, and I feared that my worst nightmare was about to become reality. I would be eaten by the bull. After the animal passed, she realized that it was one of the milking herd that had escaped, and we returned to her house in safety. In light of my childhood history, I have no idea why I was so drawn to Little Red.

When Little Red was born, the farmer was a child and he recalled sitting on the animal's back and playing bull-rider with his friends. The bull was not tethered, and every so often he would

escape, and terrified monastery guests would sound the alarm: "There's a bull in the yard! Someone come and deal with him!" The farmer would be called and one of the monks, who had dealt with many of Little Red's escapes, would go outside and talk to him, sometimes managing to get a rope through his nose ring. Little Red was always obedient to his owner and always ready for another attempt at freedom. One morning, a teenaged guest had offered to help with work in the grounds and was sent into the woods behind the house where a chain link fence enclosed a small cemetery. Weeds needed to be cleared and some garbage had found its way into the enclosure. The guest did not show up for lunch, and later in the afternoon a monk went to see how he was doing with his task. He found the terrified teenager standing in the middle of the enclosure with the gate closed while Little Red walked around the outside curiously nudging at the fence with his head.

One day, the farmer approached me when Little Red came to the fence to be scratched. "Please don't pet him any more," the farmer said. "I've been noticing a change in his behavior, a much more aggressive attitude, and the fence is insubstantial. The cows are calving and that can make him unpredictable." The message was also delivered to the monks, including Father Ray, who often rode his bicycle through the trails and pastures. He was warned to stay out of the grazing field where Little Red, cows, and calves were located. Sadly, Father Ray did not heed the warning. He was found by a farm employee one afternoon, lying face down on the ground next to his buckled bicycle, surrounded by Little Red and the herd. An autopsy revealed a severed aorta probably caused by a blunt blow to the chest. Whether Little Red had playfully butted him or aggressively attacked, we will never know, but we were all stunned to learn of Father Ray's untimely death. The loss of Father Ray brought deep grief to the community. At his funeral the Superior said, "Raymond was always a surprise." And he was.

We all experience loss. How we deal with losing a job, loved one, health, or home is determined by how we choose to live day by day. In 2004, natural disasters led many to doubt the presence of God, and some misguided and insensitive preachers represented those calamities as God's judgment on sinful people and places. We need to lament when life brings pain and loss, not to announce judgment or utter platitudes. In times of loss, faith is tested and also strengthened as we learn to trust God with our anguish. As I listened to the heart-rending cries of those who lost homes and loved ones when Hurricane Katrina crashed ashore along the Gulf Coast in September 2005, I recall the words of one New Orleans woman who had lost everything: "I didn't lose the Lord! I don't understand what has happened, and I weep for all the losses, but this I know: God has promised never to leave or forsake me, so somehow we will get through all this together."

The Hebrew Scriptures and Judaism have much to teach us about crying out in anguish, questioning God, and expressing our grief in solitude and in community rituals. Jeremiah, a prophet who suffered verbal and physical abuse for his proclamation of God's truth, sees terrible devastation in the land he loves and says:

> *My joy is gone, grief is upon me, my heart is sick. Hark,*
> *the cry of my poor people from far and wide in the land. "Is*

*the Lord not in Zion? . . . The harvest is past, the summer
is ended, and we are not saved." For the hurt of my poor
people I am hurt, I mourn, and dismay has taken hold of
me. Is there no balm in Gilead? Is there no physician
there? Why then has the health of my poor people not been
restored? . . . O that my head were a spring of water, and
my eyes a fountain of tears, so that I might weep day and
night for the slain of my poor people! (Jeremiah 8:18–9:1)*

Many of the psalms are laments recited by the community or by
a lone sufferer:

*O God, you have rejected us, broken our defenses; you have
been angry; now restore us!" (Psalm 60:1); "By the waters
of Babylon—there we sat down and there we wept when
we remembered Zion. On the willows there we hung up
our harps. For there our captors asked us for songs, and our
tormentors asked for mirth, saying, "Sing us one of the
songs of Zion!" How could we sing the Lord's song in a
foreign land?" (Psalm 137:1–4). "I cry aloud to God,
aloud to God, that he may hear me. In the day of my
trouble I seek the Lord; in the night my hand is stretched
out without wearying; my soul refuses to be comforted.
I think of God, and I moan; I meditate, and my spirit
faints" (Psalm 77:1–3).*

We are not expected to be Pollyana people because we have faith
in God. God invites us to be real: to express our pain, doubt, and
fear; to mourn and lament our losses and to acknowledge that sometimes we doubt that our faith will ever be restored. Jesus shows us
the way when, fromthe cross, he cries out "My God, my God, why
have you forsaken me?," giving voice to Psalm 22:1.

The community mourned Father Raymond's death, but his
funeral was a glorious celebration of a resurrection life, with the
telling of many stories about his eccentric escapades. We missed him
and I missed Little Red. Happily, the bull was not slaughtered but

sent to a distant farm where he continued to enjoy his promiscuous and protective role with a new herd of cows.

REFLECTING WITH SCRIPTURE
Luke 24:1–35
How do you deal with loss? Consider writing your own psalm to express personal or community losses and disappointment with God

PRAYER
Sometimes I feel discouraged, mired in a pit of despair. O God come to my aid; hear the wailing of my heart as I cry out to you "Why? Why? Why did this happen to me? Where are you when I suffer?" I refuse to listen to false comforters, but I take shelter in you even when I do not feel your presence, for you have said that you never leave or forsake me. Help me, God. Amen.

LETHARGY

Narcotic Naps

I met Oprah on July 31, 1997. She was a shy creature but very sleepy, so she did not protest when I took her into my arms. One huge ear brushed my face and her clawed arm rested on my shoulder. She turned her face anxiously toward the assistant who cared for her in the wildlife sanctuary, perhaps looking for reassurance as she rested in the arms of a stranger. Oprah had been orphaned before she came to the center and, like the other koalas who had been rescued, could not have survived in the wild. Koala habitat has been diminished, and many animals have died on the highways that now cross the Australian outback, so it is rare to see one of these creatures in their natural setting, Leaving Brisbane in the morning, I had traveled to the wildlife center by river boat, and during the hour-long trip, we saw many colorful birds as well as huge colonies of fruit-bats, also known as flying foxes. Just inside the center, tame kangaroos approached us hoping for food, and several emus strutted self-importantly a short distance away. But it was the koalas that I had especially hoped to see, and now Oprah was nestled in my arms.

Koalas are not bears, but one of the multitude of marsupials found in Australia. They carry their young in a pouch and live in the branches of eucalyptus trees, whose leaves form their primary diet. But there is a problem: the leaves of the eucalyptus are also a

narcotic, so koalas eat, then fall asleep, eat some more, and fall asleep, while firmly anchored in the tree tops. I watched one female with her baby tucked into her pouch munching ever more slowly until her eyes closed, her head dropped, and she became unaware of my presence. I learned that koalas spend as much as twenty-three hours a day sleeping.

For the koala, frequently falling asleep is natural, and I must confess that a nap in the afternoon is very appealing to me too. I remember how my father, after work, would sit down in an easy

chair, light his pipe, and a few minutes later be snoring loudly. The
pipe often fell from his open mouth and burned holes in his
sweaters. After a cold day of leaf raking or some other activity that
leads to a healthy tiredness, it is inviting to sit by the fire with a
book, and inevitably we "nod off."

Naps are good, restorative, and luxurious—but humans are not
meant to live in a state of narcolepsy. Sometimes we are drugged by
the compulsion to make more money, seek fame, overeat or drink, or
with obsession with the latest fad, all of which can leave us physical-
ly, mentally, and spiritually exhausted. Then it is all too easy to fall
asleep to the wonderful reality of Holy Presence in a world of grace.
The Christian tradition has a word that describes this attitude of
forgetfulness: *Accidie* is a state of spiritual sloth or indifference and
one that was especially abhorrent to the early desert hermits. They
recognized that a life of discipline was essential if they were not to
succumb to the temptations of boredom, the satisfying of diversion-
ary appetites, or falling prey to the moral turpitude that often invaded their thoughts. As I read their stories, I am aware that they were
no different from ourselves, and that choosing a life of solitude and
prayer did not deliver them from accidie.

Paul writes to the Christians in Rome, urging them:

> *It is now the moment for you to wake from sleep. For
> salvation is nearer to us now than when we became
> believers; the night is far gone, the day is near. Let us then
> lay aside the works of darkness and put on the armor of
> light; let us live honorably as in the day, not in reveling
> and drunkenness, not in debauchery and licentiousness,
> not in quarreling and jealousy. Instead put on the Lord
> Jesus Christ, and make no provision for the flesh, to
> gratify its desires. (Romans 13:11–14)*

Putting on Christ is like donning armor against the sleepiness
that causes us to forget our call to live faithfully with a commitment
to self-discipline. Jesus also emphasizes the need for watchfulness:
"Keep awake therefore, for you do not know on what day your Lord
is coming" (Matthew 24:42). The context of this verse is the coming

of the Son of Man at the end of the age, but it has a much broader significance. Christ is always coming to us in our times of prayer, daily work, relationships, and in the natural world, but we will not see him unless we are awake. And we will only stay awake if we are consistent in those daily disciplines that alert us to Christ's presence. In the mornings we commit ourselves into God's hands, but do we remember to stay watchful as the day unfolds? How do we stay awake? One of the great blessings of the years I lived in a monastery was the regularity of the bell that called us to worship. Now I have to work much harder to remember in the midst of telephone calls, deadlines, and pastoral needs to pause, be still for a few moments in order to see God, who is right there in my busyness.

We Western Christians tend to think of sin in terms of the things we have done and left undone. In the Eastern Church, one of the definitions of sin is "to be asleep." The icons in an Orthodox church are not simply decorations, but invitations for the worshiper to enter the story they convey and to wake up to God, visible among us. Perhaps an important question to consider is: "What helps me to wake up to God?" Examples may include listening to music, walking in nature, engaging in creativity, eating a meal, entering a church for a few minutes in the middle of a long day, sitting with an elderly neighbor who is lonely. Scheduling a day of retreat with the purpose of asking God to reveal areas of sleepiness may help and also lead to a fresh commitment to those spiritual disciplines that help keep us attentive and awake.

Koalas are wonderful animals to observe but not to emulate. When they nod off, it is a natural response to their eating habits and environment; they are living their koala-fullness. We are members of the family of God and followers of Christ, who urges us to stay awake like those who are ready for action. The enervating fog of accidie will, from time to time, engulf us, but like the spiritual athletes of the desert, we keep returning to the love and forgiveness of God. In a passage that calls upon Christians to renounce the evil ways of their culture, we hear this imperative: "Sleeper, awake! Rise from the dead, and Christ will shine on you" (Ephesians 5:14). Today we pray for the grace to wake up to God's call to make Christ visible in the world.

REFLECTING WITH SCRIPTURE
Matthew 26:36–46
How do you practice mindfulness? Do you recall times when you have been awakened to God's presence in fresh ways?

PRAYER
Loving God and Shepherd, we give thanks for the promise that you watch over us and that you neither slumber nor sleep. Keep us alert to you in difficult times and in times of rest. Open our eyes to see your presence in the world about us and help us to respond with compassion to our neighbors, so that they too may be awakened to your love. Amen.

DILIGENCE

Outback High–Rise

"The ants are a people without strength, yet they provide their food in summer."—Proverbs 30:25

Anyone who has watched ants busy on a newly swept patio cannot help but admire their diligence as they work together carrying loads sometimes twice their own size. Ants also surprise us with their ingenuity and ability to find sources of sweetness in cupboards, on kitchen counters, and wherever small, sticky fingers have left their mark. Ants and termites are industrious creatures willing to rebuild many times when their nests are disturbed. Earlier in the book of Proverbs we read:

> *Go to the ant you, lazybones; consider its ways, and be wise. Without having any chief or officer or ruler, it prepares food in summer, and gathers its sustenance in harvest. How long will you lie there, O lazybones? When will you rise from your sleep? A little sleep, a little slumber, a little folding of the hands to rest, and poverty will come upon you like a robber, and want, like an armed warrior.* (Proverbs 6:6–11).

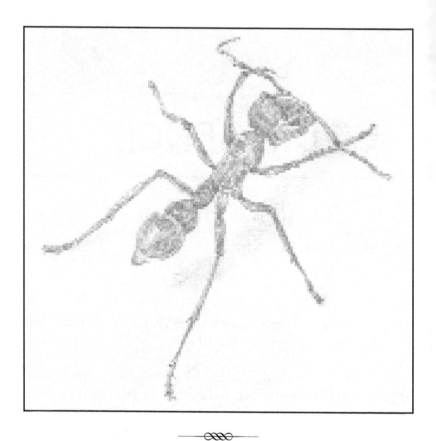

In this passage the people are urged to go and observe the ant as an example of wisdom and industry. Like the ant, they are to provide food for their families throughout the year, refusing the inclination to laziness.

Every three months, Bill the bug man comes to my house to check on the presence of ants and other unwelcome guests. During the past summer, Bill paid two extra visits because the ant population seemed to be reaching plague proportions. There were flying ants in the upstairs bedrooms—I learned that only the females grew wings—while male armies were attacking every possible surface in my kitchen. "It's a bad year everywhere," Bill told me as he sprayed toxic chemicals in nooks and crannies where the ants liked to hide. I pulled out some photographs to share with Bill and said: "If you think we have problems, take a look at these." I had been to Australia, and in the outback we had come upon termite mounds that reached several feet above my head. Unlike the small anthills we sometimes destroy in our yards, the termites went on building year after year undisturbed, and their high-rise condominiums reached ever further toward the sky. The termites were just as busy as the ants I watched at home, only these were very pale-bodied insects carrying loads upward rather than across the surface. Strangely, though ants and termites work busily, they do not seem as frantic as many of us who rush from place to place with anxious faces and heartburn, only to collapse with exhaustion at the end of the day. Our frenetic lives rarely seem to be satisfying, and it is our health and families that are neglected in the race to success.

My grandmother was diligent even in her later years when physical movement was limited. She hand-sewed simple garments like aprons, she crocheted, and she knitted. Nan's industriousness blessed her extended family with gifts each birthday and Christmas. These inexpensive items were greatly valued because we knew how much loving care had gone into creating them. Nan would sit in her upright chair with the project in her lap and only occasionally take a nap. There was no TV, but she did sometimes listen to the old accumulator-operated radio, which stood on a small table close to her slightly deaf ear. She also loved murder mysteries and could spend an hour or two caught up in a story from one of the books Mother picked for her from the local library. Years before, when Nan's husband died in an accident, she became a single mother of five young children. A sixth boy had been killed in a road accident, and life was very hard for poor families in the early years of the twentieth century. But Nan's diligence and hard work enabled the family to survive and set a pattern for her children to follow.

When someone asks me "How are you?," I often find myself telling the questioner how busy I am and how difficult it is to take time out. I justify my existence by telling others that I am overworked, in demand and longing for some time off. There is frenetic pride in my response, and it reveals that I am a child of the age where goal-oriented busyness is the norm. Is this the kind of diligence that the author of Proverbs had in mind when he suggested that ants have lessons for humankind? I suspect not. The word diligence (*diligentem*) means to love and select as well as to be industrious. We cannot always select the kind of work we do, but we can choose how we will go about our tasks. Diligence suggests faithful attention to work and the avoidance of short cuts that may compromise the quality of a task. Diligence implies single-mindedness, attention to detail, and a realization that others will be blessed or inconvenienced by the way in which we go about a task.

Some years ago, I read a story about the struggles of an Englishwoman who felt called to become a Buddhist priest. She had to deal with ethnic, language, and gender issues, and it was a long hard struggle to win support and acceptance. She was given many humiliating tasks to do in order to discourage her from her path. One evening, the monks were invited out to a celebration, and she was left behind to clean up and wash all the dishes they had used that day. She experienced a boiling resentment, for she too had been looking forward to the event. Then she remembered a key teaching from her tradition: mindfulness. She had work to do that she could accomplish with anger and self-pity, or with loving attention. She had a choice. The young novice chose attention, washing the dishes with appreciation for their shape, color, beauty, and usefulness, and she remembered her community and the importance of clean plates and cups. The task became a work of love and marked the moment of enlightenment for her as a moment of joy and awareness of the sacredness of the most lowly work. Buddhist wisdom suggests, "If you are picking cranberries, pick cranberries," but the diligence implied in the statement goes beyond one particular faith tradition. It is there in the Hebrew Scriptures as we have seen, and Paul writes about how Christians build on the foundation laid by Christ: "Each builder must choose with care how to build. . . . with gold, silver, precious stones, wood, hay, straw—the work of each builder will become visible" (1 Corinthians 3:10, 12–13). How extraordinary it would be to see ants running round in circles but accomplishing little, hiding in a corner while others carried burdens, or stopping to tell each other what hard workers they were. These pesky little creatures will be our teachers if we let them.

REFLECTING WITH SCRIPTURE
Matthew 7:24–27
Can you recall people who have been examples of diligence for you?
How might you become more attentive to tasks and responsibilities?

PRAYER
Creator God, we see your work in the beauty of nature and in the
lives of friends and family. Help us to be attentive to the tasks you
set before us, knowing that in serving others we are serving you. May
we consider no act of service too small or distasteful to demand our
full and willing attention. As Christ washed the feet of his disciples,
may we stoop to honor the sacredness of our brothers and sisters and
so help them to know their belovedness in God's eyes and ours.
Amen.

COMPANIONSHIP

Big Ben

A single-track dirt road leads deep into the mountains of northern California. My rental car groans as we navigate rocks, steep inclines, and deep ruts, and I begin to wonder if I misunderstood directions. There is no sign of life or human habitation, and I begin to imagine that, years later, someone will find the rusted-out vehicle with my bones decaying within it. At last I cross another mountain pass and descend through dense woodland toward a scattering of ranch buildings and the hope of a good meal. I am not disappointed. After being shown to my A-frame cabin, I am welcomed into the dining room, where the home-cooked dinner includes a lavish supply of organic vegetables, grown on the ranch. Year-round residents welcome me for my week of retreat and the director's chocolate brown Labrador scarcely contains his excitement. As I return to my cabin for the night, I pass the in-ground spa and determine that tomorrow I will luxuriate in the hot water after a hike in the hills.

It has been a long day. Two plane trips, a bus ride to Santa Anna, and then a stressful drive to the ranch have left their mark, and I am ready to fall into bed, giving thanks for safe arrival and anticipating time to "be." I am just drifting into sleep when a sound outside the door brings me back to full consciousness, and when it persists, I reluctantly get out of bed to investigate. Outside the door, Ben, the

chocolate lab, looks up at me wagging his tail, inviting me out to play. "Tomorrow" I say, "if it is okay with your owner, we'll go for a walk." Ben is even more excited, probably interpreting my words as an immediate response to his desire, so again I repeat "tomorrow," and after patting him, I go back to bed. In the morning I have forgotten about Ben until I open my door. He has spent the night on the doormat and now barks and turns circles, making sure I am ready to keep my promise.

Each year I spend a week of retreat and usually choose a monastic house where the regular prayers or "offices" provide a rhythm for my own reflection. Somehow, as I prayed about where to go that year, God seemed to be inviting me out of regular structures that I find comfortable, and into nature. I left my prayer book behind and prayed for the grace to listen, look, and wait for the Spirit to show me the way. Ben came in answer to that prayer. After breakfast we set off, hiking up to the ridge top through vegetation that was pungent but unfamiliar to me. Several times, curious rabbits crossed our path and I lost sight of Ben as he raced after them, but he always returned to check on my progress. The only human-generated sounds I heard were distant felling of trees and an occasional jet high above us. Birdsong was everywhere and many tracks, unrecognizable to me but of deep interest to Ben, zigzagged between the rocks. When I finally puffed my way onto the ridge, red-tailed hawks wheeled and cried above us as I sat on a rock filled with wordless wonder and delight. Ben joined me to rest a while, and I shared some cookies with him. This holy moment, and many more that followed, remain in my memory as gracious, holy gifts.

We all need companions on our journey, and sometimes they will be four-legged friends. For the seven days of my retreat, Ben became my companion-friend and taught me how to be in the moment, to express joy, to trust in his wisdom when I was lost, and to discover the exuberance of life lived to the full. My other companion was my journal, in which I reflected on the experiences of each day. Gradually, I came to the awareness that I had moved out of my head and into my body; Ben's example was truly incarnational, for he embodied holy joy. At the end of each day, my body ached, but my heart was full, for I had seen God in the wildness of hawks, crags, and tiny flowers that bloomed despite the intense dryness. And I especially met God in my faithful friend who led me safely even through a raging thunderstorm that frightened him and me.

Those who gathered around Jesus were taught many lessons about companionship, though often they were reluctant to receive his teaching. Sometimes they wanted to argue about hierarchy and who was the most important (Matthew 18:1–6), and Jesus placed a child among them and said that they must change and become like children. Children are naturally spontaneous, curious, in touch with their feelings, and in love with life. "Be like that," says Jesus. "Be like Ben," I think to myself when I become too orderly, settled in my understanding, and caught up with "head stuff," and when life becomes tedious. As he prepared to leave the disciples, Jesus showed them how to be companions to one another by loving as he loved and serving as he served. Chapters thirteen to seventeen of the Gospel according to John contain many reassurances about life in the community of faith beyond the physical presence of Jesus. The disciples had not come together because they particularly liked each other—in fact, their diverse personalities were likely to create difficulties—but they were companions by reason of their relationship with Christ. The church today is just as diverse, and sometimes we miss finding companions there because we prejudge people. Someone has a different view of politics, theology, material possessions, or the choir, and we exclude them from our circle of companions, forgetting that our bond is Jesus Christ. We might nod politely or say hello at coffee hour, but we fail to see that person as a companion with gifts that will help us grow spiritually. Just a few moments of paying attention, listening to another, may lead to the discovery of fresh insights and vitality that lead to a deep relationship.

I have been known to say, "I'm really a cat person," and I don't readily warm to dogs who want to leap all over me and lick my face before we have really met each other, but over the years I have celebrated wonderful dog companions. Our bitch Sally, who gave birth to puppies on an old sack of grain, was a dear friend for many years, and Gyp, shaggy haired and very loveable, inherited her place in our family. Max, the black lab who lived with us at the monastery, would walk for miles with me and was also a wonderful companion to my cat Bonnie. The two of them would curl up in the sun on the porch for an afternoon nap. And I am so glad that Ben came to me as a companion at a time when I needed to relax and let go of routine for a while, so that I could celebrate the gifts of spontaneity and freedom.

Reflecting with Scripture
Luke 19:1–10
Who are your companions? Do you recall companions who came into your life for a short time yet blessed you immeasurably? Are there any in your community who might enable you to see in new ways if you embraced their companionship?

Prayer
Thank you, loving God, for companions who come into our lives,

bringing newness. Open our hearts to spontaneity and play and show us where our routines have deprived us of life in its fullness. Show us how those we dismiss as different may become our close companions if we are willing to reach out and to trust them. May your Spirit be our companion, reminding us that Jesus called his disciples friends and loved each of them despite their differences. And may we especially be ready to respond to the wisdom of our four-legged companions who love us beyond measure. Amen.

JOY

Singin' in the Rain

Under a huge oak tree above Glendalough's twin lakes in the Wicklow Mountains of Ireland, the would-be hermit Kevin built a tiny dwelling for himself. Earlier he had lived in an inaccessible cave high in the rock face above the lake. A monastic village was built to house monks who chose to follow Kevin and included many local people and their cattle. But the saint longed for solitude. The cell he built was very narrow, allowing room only for sleep and meditation, in keeping with the Celtic monastic ideal of simplicity and asceticism. When Kevin assumed the traditional prayer posture of standing with arms outspread in cruciform style, it was necessary to allow one arm to pass through the window. Once, when the saint stood praying, a blackbird spotted his open hand and decided it would be an ideal place to lay her eggs. When Kevin realized what had happened, he determined to maintain the posture until the eggs were hatched.

Stories about the Celtic saints frequently contain animal tales that point to the close relationship between humans and the whole created order. The Celts did not make a separation between creation and themselves, between this world and the world to come, between the living and departed. There is always an important truth hidden in accounts of the close relationship between Celtic people and the

animals. In the story of Kevin and the blackbird, we learn of the deep respect the saint had for such a tiny, joyous bird. Kevin showed patience, compassion, and selfless care for the little ones of God's creating, and perhaps there is also a hint of Kevin's sense of delight and joy, for the blackbird of the British Isles has the most beautiful song. She is a shy bird, usually hidden in woodland areas, and about the size of a starling. Her glossy feathers shine, though not with the deep black color of her mate who also sports a yellow ochre bill.

In the lanes and woodlands of Hertfordshire, where I grew up, my siblings and I would listen for the blackbird when we walked with my mother in spring. Of course, we always carried waterproof clothing because the weather in Britain is unpredictable. My mother was a wonderful teacher, telling us the names of hedgerow flowers and joining in our playful imaginations as we rambled across ploughed fields and waded streams. Often, we would be caught in a shower. Waterproofs were pulled on, and we would dance in the quickly forming puddles, mother included. And then we would hear it—the joyful, clear-throated song of the blackbird. She would be at the end of a branch, raindrops glistening on her feathers and head thrown back as she sounded forth the blessing of rain. When I recall the song of the blackbird, I also smell the damp, fresh earth, feel the exhilaration of childhood play, and touch the prickly wild rose bush with its delicate pink flowers. Blackbirds love to sing in the rain and they show me the meaning of joy.

Jesus tells his disciples that their relationship with him is like that of a vine to its branches. They will live fruitful lives if they stay connected to him, their source of nourishment and growth, though from time to time they will experience painful pruning by God, the vinegrower. Then he says to them: "I have said these things to you so that my joy may be in you, and that your joy may be complete" (John 15:11). Above all, Jesus wants to share his joy with those who followed him. Joy is more than happiness, satisfaction, or warm, fuzzy feelings. Joy is the deep trust in God's unfailing love that sustains us through dreary days as well as times when the blackbird sings. A childhood song I no longer fully remember contained the words: "Happiness happens, but joy abides in the heart that is stayed on Jesus." Jesus wants us to have complete joy, to be like children dancing in the puddles, delighting in spontaneous play, letting our lives unfold into beautiful, fruit-bearing creativity.

A thread of joy runs through the Bible like golden yarn in a tapestry. The Psalms alone contain thirty-seven references to joy and joyfulness. In Psalm 16:11 are words almost identical to those of Jesus: "In your presence there is fullness of joy; in your right hand are pleasures forevermore." Again and again, people are called upon to be joyful because joy honors God: "Come, let us sing to the Lord; let us make a joyful noise to the rock of our salvation! Let us come into (God's) presence with thanksgiving; let us make a joyful noise to him with songs of praise!" (Psalm 95:1–2). The return of God's people to their homeland is predicted in Isaiah: "So the ransomed of the Lord shall return, and come to Zion with singing; everlasting joy shall be upon their heads; they shall obtain joy and gladness, and sorrow and sighing shall flee away" (Isaiah 51:11). God's purpose for humankind is joy, fullness of life, and an ever-deepening relationship with the Creator who looks at us and says "It is very good!" (Genesis 1:31).

Some of the most joy-filled people I have known have lived their joy through times of great suffering. An elderly woman confined most of the time to her bed due to numerous health problems was always an inspiration when I visited her. She kept a box of index cards close at hand and daily prayed for each person and situation named on the cards. Intercessory prayer was her ministry. I never heard her complain or talk much about herself; she always had a smile, maintained her deep interest in others, and spoke joyfully about God's goodness. Seven women living with AIDS formed a singing group in their township near Johannesburg and made a commitment to each other to care for the children when one of them died. They embodied joy, and their music brought hope to many. A thirteen-year-old boy diagnosed with leukemia refused to give up hope. He asked for full details of his prognosis and treatment, lived through the nausea and debilitation of chemotherapy, and always had a smile for those who visited him in the hospital. After a long, slow recovery, the disease is now in remission, and when he was able to return to school, he worked tirelessly to raise money for other children suffering from cancer. I watched him on the local news program—a bald, smiling teenager who embodied joy.

Joy resides deep in the heart of God's people; it is where they are at home. Isaiah said that in coming home, joy would be abundant, everlasting. Perhaps we lose our sense of joy when we are preoccupied with busyness, forgetful of our need to stay connected with Christ the Vine through daily disciplines of prayer and presence. Perhaps we stray from the heart of joy when we get more excited about differences in theology than in the worship of God, or when we allow disappointment and fear to overwhelm. The blackbird calls us to come home to joy as she sings beneath gray skies and falling rain.

REFLECTING WITH SCRIPTURE
1 Peter 1:3–9
When have you experienced fullness of joy? Have you met people who have lived their joy in the midst of pain? How will you stay connected to Christ the Vine so that your joy will continue to flourish?

PRAYER
God of joy and homecoming, when we stray from you, you call us back. May your voice be to us as the golden notes of the blackbird who celebrates the gift of rain and a place to rest. Our hope is in you, the Source and Sustainer of our lives. Amen.

SOLITUDE

Red Riding Hood Got It Wrong

I grew up listening to the Mowgli stories in Rudyard Kipling's *Jungle Book*. My mother was a fine storyteller, and I loved the jungle world of my imagination. That world was filled with breathtaking delight as I listened again and again to the story of a lost infant raised by wolves. Mowgli learned to live like wolves, to honor the laws of the jungle, and to obey his great friend and teacher, Balloo the bear. Sheer Kahn the tiger, who claimed that Mowgli was his, made numerous attempts on the life of the child, but Mowgli's protectors kept him from death, often at great cost to themselves. The animated cartoon version of the story fell far short of the spine-tingling tale I heard as a child when my mother took on each of the characters as she read the story. Kipling was not the first to tell of lost infants protected by wolves, but his version, set in India during the time of the Raj, was vibrantly alive to me, and I have loved wolves ever since.

Wolves are generally community oriented and live in packs dominated by an alpha male, but from time to time, a lone wolf will leave the family group. This was the case in the movie *Dances with Wolves*, where Dunbar, played by Kevin Costner, is befriended by a lone wolf. The image of a single wolf howling before a full moon is a familiar one, and we use the epithet "lone wolf" to describe some-

one who is very independent, maybe standoffish, and who spurns social occasions or close relationships with others. We are not certain why a wolf leaves the pack, sometimes for a short time of solitude, but perhaps it needs the time and space to regroup or test its ability to survive alone. I do know that I need times of solitude, times of withdrawal in order to listen to the wisdom within and to listen to God. The endless words, commercial pressures, busyness, expectations, and my inclination to press on come what may, tend to make me deaf to the truth of who I am and to neglect the voice of the Holy One who is trying to get a word in edgewise. When I finally recognize what is going on, I know that it is time to withdraw from the pack for a while.

One of my favorite places to go for a short time away from my busy computer and church community is the Asheville Nature

Center, where red wolves have been successfully bred and released into the wild. These shy creatures are not always easy to see, and sometimes I will sit on a bench and wait for a long time just to get a glimpse of one of them. The babies are especially delightful and a little less reclusive than the parents. Sitting, waiting, becoming centered, I find that my body begins to relax, my mind rests, and my spirit is renewed. Sometimes a party of school children will pass, but their chatter and excitement are less an invasion of my solitude than an invitation to allow my imagination and delight to be engaged. Next to the red wolf enclosure is a small pack of gray wolves who sometimes rest close to the protective fence. One day, as I watched the gray wolves, an ambulance, siren wailing, passed by the wooded area just below the nature center. The wolves all threw back their heads and howled. I enjoyed a glorious private symphony, and they did not seem to mind when I joined in their song.

Jesus was aware of the need for solitude, and took every opportunity he could to withdraw from the crowds in order to be with God. Sometimes his time alone was disturbed. In Mark 1:35–40, we read of the disciples going out early in the morning to find Jesus who was praying in a deserted place. "Everyone is searching for you," they said, implying that he needed to leave the place of prayer and go back down into the city, but Jesus replied that it was time to move on. I suspect that Jesus might have recalled his time of temptation in the wilderness when he confronted the human desire to gain popularity by being spectacular. He could so easily have returned to the place of successful ministry, but in the time of solitude with God, he found the strength to honor his mission to take the good news beyond that locality. "Let us go on to the neighboring towns, so that I may proclaim the message there also; for that is what I came out to do" (1:38). Discernment of God's call and faithfulness to the gospel is supported by the discipline of withdrawal from others into a solitude that gives hospitality to the Spirit of God, who makes clear the truth about ourselves and our call to serve. On another occasion, when the disciples are filled with excitement as they returned from a mission trip, Jesus interrupts their recital of all the great things that had happened and says: "Come away to a deserted place all by yourselves and rest a while" (Mark 6:31).

Withdrawal from even the most successful ministry is sometimes necessary to avoid the temptation to be so caught up in enthusiastic sharing of the news that we forget to listen to God.

The early desert mothers and fathers knew the importance of solitude in order to live the gospel in a very intentional way. These men and women of the early Christian centuries left the cities in order to embrace a very simple life of prayer, and they soon became wise guides for others, who came to them seeking help on the Christian journey. The life of solitude was a blessing to many, but it soon became clear that the hermits also needed contact with a community of faith. Monasteries were formed so that the hermits themselves might find more balance by some worship and activities undertaken in common. Today, monks are discouraged from becoming permanent solitaries, and in most communities only the most experienced and faithful members will be granted permission to withdraw entirely from the community, though all monastics are encouraged to take times of solitude during each year. Have you ever been to a monastery? Many offer space for guests to claim some solitude as well as guidance from community members who know how difficult it is to give ourselves time to listen to God. Even if a short time away from work or family is not possible, an intentional hour or two when we take the phone of the hook and choose a space at home where we can be in solitude can be a wonderful interlude of holy listening.

A good friend of mine, also a lover of wolves, attended a program where an injured wolf who could not be rehabilitated in the wild had become tame enough to be taken to schools and other community centers to educate people about the beauty and gentleness of wolves. My friend arrived early at the center and found a seat on the front row. She was awed to be so close to the wolf, and after its handler had taken it round the room, the wolf lay down at the front of the room with its beautiful head resting on my friend's foot. Gone were all the myths of terror about wolves, the Red Riding Hood stories designed to frighten children. A lone wolf rested trustingly among humans, providing a metaphor for the desire God has to be with us as we rest, unafraid, in the divine presence.

Reflecting with Scripture
Mark 1:12–13

Who are the members of your pack? Have you ever chosen some time of solitude away from familiar companions in order to listen to your life? What do you fear most about stepping outside routine and comfortable relationships?

Prayer

Listening God, hear me when I howl; touch me when I am afraid; give me courage to step out into the unknown so that I may know you and know myself in the wild beauty of relationship. Amen.

INGENUITY

Two Lovely Black Eyes

In the small hours of the morning, I woke with a start, thinking I had heard sounds of a break-in. I held my breath and listened hard: nothing. It must have been a dream, I thought, and I was drifting back to sleep when a very loud crash brought me to full consciousness. This time I could distinguish sounds of a scuffle, so I got up quickly and switched on lights. Cautiously I went to the window after snatching up the hand-held telephone, but there was no sign of intruders in the yard. Finally, I was able to detect that the noise was coming from the screen porch, and when I looked through the glass panes in the door, I saw the culprit. A large raccoon had found a tiny tear in the screen—a tear I had been intending to repair for some time—and had ripped the mesh into a hole large enough for him to pass through. The raccoon had detected the presence of birdseed, which I kept in a large plastic container on the porch. The bin was now overturned, and what was left of the seed scattered over the concrete floor. I opened the house door, and the raccoon fled to the far end of the porch, attempted to climb the mesh, but tumbled back down and hid behind garden furniture. I needed to invite my nocturnal thief to leave, but wary of rabies, did not want to confront him directly, so I stepped onto the porch just far enough to throw open the door that would allow him access into the yard and the

woods from which he had doubtless come. Retreating back into the house, I watched as he left his hiding place, took one look at the open doorway, and exited through the hole by which he had entered.

This was my first encounter with the local raccoon population. Very early in the morning several months later, I let my cat out and went to put on the coffee. Almost at once, sounds of a catfight pierced the quiet, pre-birdsong morning, and I ran outside expecting to rescue Bonnie, who was routinely beaten up by the neighbor's much larger feline. Instead, I found that she was in a stand off with a female raccoon; both were uttering blood curdling threats, but the raccoon ran off into the woods when I appeared. Then I discovered the reason for her visit and willingness to stand her ground. A baby raccoon was hunkered down on the path, and as I went to pick up my cat, the little raccoon ran toward me with pitiful squeaks. It had lost its fleeing mother and was no doubt begging me for mercy and a good meal. Of course, I learned not to leave any kind of food on the porch after this, though I have several times had to clean up a scattered mess in the yard after ingenious raccoons have somehow pried off the lid of the trash can.

As humans invade more and more animal habitat, the creatures who were here before us are compelled to find new ways to survive. While humans sleep, coyotes, possums, rodents, raccoons, owls, and skunks hunt in the woods behind my house, and the bears come early in the morning or at dusk. They have learned to outwit me in the same way that daytime squirrels break through every squirrel-proof bird feeder I have ever bought. These creatures demand access to the habitat that has been theirs for centuries. God is like that too. No matter how hard we try to keep the Holy One out of our lives, God uses divine ingenuity to return again and again to reclaim the lost territory of our hearts. Isaiah portrays God speaking to Israel saying: "Now thus says the Lord . . . who created you . . . who formed you. . . . Do not fear, for I have redeemed you; I have called you by name, you are mine" (Isaiah 43:1). This tender passage continues to speak of the lengths to which God will go to rescue and sustain the people and to bring them back into intimate relationship.

The prophet Hosea writes of God's love for Israel, of God calling them home: "I led them with cords of human kindness, with bands of love. I was to them like those who lift infants to their cheeks. I bent down to them and fed them" (Hosea 11:4). In compassion, God searches for those who forget their true home, pleading with them to return, to come out from their fortified dwellings and to risk the wild, natural place that is home. And God uses ingenuity to wake us up. Under cover of darkness God visits us in our sleepy state of being and startles us into awareness. "You have forgotten that I belong here with you, that I want to share your home and hospitality. I will find even the tiniest place of your vulnerability and will make myself small enough to enter your outer space and wait outside your locked door. And I'll make a bit of noise to let you know I am there."

In a series of letters addressed to early Christians in seven Asian churches, God pleads with disciples to return home. To the church in Laodicea, God says: "Listen! I am standing at the door, knocking; if you hear my voice and open the door, I will come in to you and eat with you and you with me" (Revelation 3:20). This text has been used often as an evangelistic tool, but the words are addressed to Christians who have grown lukewarm in their faith, who have forgotten to invite Christ to share their hospitality. God does not force an entry, but will use ingenious ways to alert sleepy Christians to the divine presence, and gentle knocking may sometimes be replaced by noisy crashing around outside.

A priest I knew in London served as chaplain to a boys' high school where students were encouraged to attend chapel each morning. One of his altar boys, who had faithfully shown up to serve whenever he was scheduled, began to "forget" his commitments and then disappeared from chapel services altogether. One afternoon, the chaplain encountered the student in a hallway and said to him, "Hi, Paul, where have you been? You seem to be keeping God at arm's length these days." Paul was an honest kid and without missing a beat replied, "Oh no, sir, not at arm's length, that's far too close!"

Most of the time I forget about the wildlife around me in the woods and mountains, but every once in a while they remind me of their presence and their prior claim on the land. A raccoon crashes around on my porch, a possum is attracted by sweetness on some bottles I have placed outside for recycling, a bear comes to check out the bird feeder, and I am reminded that they used to be at home here. My hospitality toward these creatures means accepting their presence and, like my Native American friends, acknowledging the gifts that four-legged brothers and sisters bring. They bring me delight, though I respect their distance, and I allow them to remind me that Christ is waiting for an invitation to come in and feast with me—to come really close—so that we can be at home together.

REFLECTING WITH SCRIPTURE
1 Samuel 3:2–10
Do you recall times when you have been startled into an awareness that God is nearby? What causes you to become "lukewarm" in your faith?

PRAYER
Patient God, please use your ingenuity to wake me up when I become sleepy in my faith. Let me hear your knock and give me courage to rouse myself and invite you in, even if I have not swept the house and put the food in the oven. May Christ be at home in my life and become visible to others through my delight in his presence. Amen.

HOMECOMING

Veldt Vespers

The sacred ibis is a silent bird. It wings its way home at twilight, its slender body etched against a vermilion sky, to roost beside the lake. A large flock gathers in the branches of a huge, leafless tree, row upon row they perch, like monks waiting for the evening service of vespers. They will keep vigil throughout the night and, at dawn, rise once more to fly over the veldt in search of food. Beside the same lake, many hadedas also spend the night. They approach the roosting site with much noise, their calls creating a cacophony of sound that tells the world "We are here and you had better pay attention to us!" Hadedas would be uncomfortable in a monastic choir. These birds communicate in a way that resembles a chattering congregation waiting for an upbeat contemporary service to begin. On a mild autumn evening, midway between Johannesburg and Pretoria, I sat on a grassy mound with a dear friend who had invited me to witness the bird homecoming. We watched as the sun slowly sank, and the sky blazed beyond a small grove of trees on the far side of the lake. We listened to the noisy hadedas and commented on the beauty of the white sacred ibis. I slowly became aware of the way in which I had already judged these birds. My preference was for the sacred ibis, a quiet bird who honors silence. My prejudice suggests that the hadedas were more like busybodies exchanging gossip at

coffee hour. The ibis is holy and mature; the hadeda worldly and shallow. I identify with the ibis and mentally tick off a list of hadedas who come to my church, or chat noisily at the table next to mine in a restaurant, or interrupt the movie I am watching with their noisy popcorn bags and stage whispers.

Reflecting further on the evening experience, though, I realize how little I know about either of these birds. I am a stranger in their homeland and I choose one characteristic, the most obvious one, on which to judge them. The quiet ones appeal to me; the noisy ones do not. My prayer and worship preferences are reflected in the birds. I would rather be a monk than a Pentecostal worshiper, a beautiful white creature rather than a dark gray one. And of course, *my* way is best!

Our human capacity to judge, discriminate, and discern is God-given. Scripture urges us to judge between good and evil, to be discriminating as we live the gospel in a world that devalues its message, and to discern the way of truth within our communities and our own hearts. But the teaching of Jesus summons us to follow him by expanding the circle of belonging. We are called to inclusivity and welcome, not to negative judgment of others. Jesus exercised judgment to unmask the posturing and hypocrisy of many seemingly devout people; he discriminated between true and false motives, between arrogant and humble attitudes, and between life-giving and death-dealing expressions of religion. And Jesus welcomed the human "hadedas" into the circle, giving them the same value he gave to those who more closely resemble the sacred ibis.

A story in the Hebrew Scriptures reveals the way in which pride and false judgment almost prevented a high-ranking military leader from finding healing. The man's name is Naaman, and though he is commander of the army, he suffers from the disease of leprosy. A young slave girl in his household knows of Elisha, a prophet who serves the God of the Hebrews and has a reputation for healing. She suggests that her master might be cured of his leprosy through Elisha. The king of Aram adds his support by writing a letter to Israel's king and sending silver, gold, and rich garments as a gift. Thinking that he is expected to heal Naaman, the king of Israel tears his clothes in distress, but Elisha hears what had happened and tells the king to send Aram's commander to him. When Naaman arrives with chariots and horses, he halts at Elisha's house, expecting the prophet to come out and heal him. He is stunned and angry when Elisha sends a messenger who says: "Go, wash in the Jordan seven times, and your flesh shall be restored and you shall be clean" (2 Kings 5:10). Furious, Naaman turns away, saying: "I thought that for me he would surely come out, and stand and call on the name of the Lord his God, and would wave his hand over the spot, and cure the leprosy. Are not Abana and Pharpar, the rivers of Damascus, better than all the waters of Israel? Could I not wash in them and be clean?" (5:11–12). Only when his servants urge him to do as Elisha has said does Naaman humble himself to bathe in the Jordan seven times, and to his amazement, he is healed.

God's grace often comes to us disguised in forms we do not easily accept. The "hadeda" moments may be pushed aside and quickly forgotten if we are not vigilant, ready to look for the holy in people and situations that are not particularly attractive. Not long ago I was in the waiting room at the hospital radiology unit, where I was scheduled for some tests. Two of us were called back to the dressing rooms to don robes, and I moved quickly so that I would be the first one ready to move on to the x-ray room. The other patient followed me out to the waiting area, but was called first to go for her x-ray. In the few moments we had sat together I had formed a negative opinion of her. I did not find her attractive. She was obese and unkempt and all too ready to start a conversation informing me in great detail about her medical history. I was very irritated when she went ahead of me, leaving me to wait; surely the staff understood how important I am, what a busy schedule I have to keep. For a few moments I looked at the blank wall opposite my chair, resentment churning away inside, until I became aware of my response. Then I began to feel deep shame. Who was I to judge the worth of another person or to assume that in a few minutes of meeting I could know anything about her? And how could I think that the world— or at least the clinic—revolved around me, giving me precedent over others? By grace I recognized my arrogant lack of compassion and was able to turn resentment into prayer for the other patient and to receive the moment as an opportunity to practice patience.

A South African evening, where gray squawking birds flew back and forth overhead and rows of silent and beautiful white birds appeared to rest in prayerful mode, offered me an invitation to look more deeply at life's daily assumptions and irritations. Hadeda days are inevitable, but I will be more able to approach them with compassionate presence if I choose to rest in silent, prayerful gratitude daily.

REFLECTING WITH SCRIPTURE
Luke 18:9–14
How might you be more intentional about taking "vespers" time each day to be still and reflect on the joys and irritations of the last twenty-four hours? Who are the hadedas of your experience? How might you pray for them?

PRAYER

Creator of white birds, gray birds, and people of many colors, give to us a right judgment in all things, and compassionate hearts to embrace diversity. Deliver us from the arrogance of self-importance, and open our hearts to your grace as it comes to us in many guises. Teach us to see your hand at work in the world around us and to give thanks always for all that you spread before us. Amen.

Printed in the USA
CPSIA information can be obtained
at www.ICGtesting.com
JSHW081442061024
71029JS00001BA/117